UNSTOPPABLE CONFIDENCE!

UNSTOPPABLE CONFIDENCE!

HOW TO USE THE
POWER OF NLP
TO BE MORE DYNAMIC AND SUCCESSFUL

KENT SAYRE
CERTIFIED NEUROLINGUISTIC PROGRAMMING TRAINER

New York   Chicago   San Francisco   Lisbon   London   Madrid   Mexico City
Milan   New Delhi   San Juan   Seoul   Singapore   Sydney   Toronto

The *McGraw·Hill* Companies

Library of Congress Cataloging-in-Publication Data

Sayre, Kent.
    Unstoppable confidence : how to use the power of NLP to be more dynamic and
successful / by Kent Sayre.
        p.   cm.
    ISBN 978-0-07-158845-4 (alk. paper)
     1. Self-confidence.   2. Success—Psychological aspects.   3. Neurolinguistic
programming.   I. Title.

BF575.S39S29   2008
158—dc22   2008005113

9 10 11 12 13 14 15 16 17 18 19 20 21 DOC/DOC 1 5 4 3

ISBN 978-0-07-158845-4
MHID   0-07-158845-0

Interior design by Monica Baziuk

McGraw-Hill books are available at special quantity discounts to use as premiums and
sales promotions or for use in corporate training programs. To contact a representative,
please visit the Contact Us pages at www.mhprofessional.com.

This book is printed on acid-free paper.

Contents

Part 3 The Language of Unstoppable Confidence

Part 4 Becoming Unstoppable

Introduction

THIS BOOK IS BOTH A product and a document of my transformation from being an extremely shy person to becoming one with a lot of confidence. I know that if I can do it,
anyone can break out of his or her shyness and become more
confident; I was truly the shyest person I had ever met! Even
if you already have a lot of confidence now, you can benefit
from this book by stretching your confidence beyond what
you thought was even possible.

My purpose for writing this book is to help everyone
who reads it immediately increase his or her confidence
through doing the exercises and adopting the philosophy
that is described throughout the book.

When I was extremely shy and lacking in confidence, I
had to take the long road to self-assurance. Through trial
and error, I've found what works, what doesn't work, and
what *really* works. Much of what works is based on the principles of neurolinguistic programming (NLP).

NLP

NLP is the study of how language, both verbal and nonverbal, affects our minds. By consciously directing our minds, we can create resourceful ways of behaving for ourselves. In this book, all of the methods are geared toward having more confidence in our lives and stepping beyond our previously defined limits.

One of the principles of NLP is that—since we all share the same neurology—whatever anyone else can do well, you can do just as well, provided that you direct your mind in exactly the same way. If confidence is possible for others (and it definitely is), it is equally possible for you too. Using NLP methods, I have constructed models of very confident people and included my behavioral research in this book. By doing what they do, you will achieve the same resourceful state of confidence that they enjoy. From the way they think to the way they talk to the way they walk, in this book you will find out how people with confidence move through the world and how the world responds.

How It Works

This book differs from the other self-help books on the shelf because it is not about theory. It is about doing what works. It is about finding what has worked for others who are confident, figuring out how to do that, and then doing it yourself. Many of the fluff motivation books on the market remind me of someone blowing up a really big balloon and then letting it go. We both know what happens to the balloon. It flies all around the room aimlessly until it returns to its original, shriveled-up shape on the ground.

Filling yourself up with motivation is great, yet motivation must ultimately come from within. There is a difference between someone telling you to "go for it!" and someone telling you to "go for it!" *and also* supplying the specific tools to do exactly that.

This book is not based on theory. It is based on proof and what really works. I'm on the street, trying this stuff out and learning from my mistakes. The beauty of this book is that you can learn from the mistakes I made in the course of doing what it took to get unstoppable confidence and prospering from my knowledge. You can take what works from this book and use it in your life. Discard what doesn't work for you. Some techniques you'll like, some you may not, and some you will love. But try it. Do the techniques and prove it to yourself!

The techniques discussed in this book are no-nonsense, street-tested, immediately applicable tools for your empowerment. I'll give you specific instructions on how and when to use these tools in your life. These techniques are so effective because they take what has worked, what does work, and what will work and break it down into small, learnable strategies that you can use to help yourself. When you learn these strategies, you will be able to duplicate the same results. At the same time, we throw away the useless techniques that have kept you stuck. I will go over the techniques that keep people stuck so you can notice whether you are engaging in one of those activities and immediately shift gears.

If you are looking for pie-in-the-sky theory, put this book down immediately! If you want to wade through a jargon-filled muddle, stop reading right now. If you want academic techniques that work only sometimes and only if you follow complicated procedures, you will not find them here.

All you will find here is unstoppable confidence!

PART 1

Getting in Gear

Why Confidence Matters

Without self-confidence we are as babes in the cradles.

—Virginia Woolf

CONFIDENCE MATTERS MORE THAN ALMOST anything else in determining your success. Therefore, it's necessary that you understand exactly how important it is.

Why Confidence Is Important

Confidence is vital because it is the difference that *makes* the difference. When people consistently take action and make the appropriate course corrections, they get massive results and achieve all their goals. However, if they lack the confidence to take action, they will stay stuck. It would be no different if they had no dreams or goals at all. After all, what's the point of wishing for anything if you don't pursue it?

Having confidence, especially when it comes to having the ability to communicate, is absolutely essential. Without it, people don't communicate effectively. The degree to which you are confident and communicate well with others is the degree to which you will succeed in life, no matter what context you're referring to: business, family, friends, career, and so on. It is directly proportional to the degree to which you will experience a rewarding and fulfilling life.

We are naturally drawn to confident people. Imagine what it would be like to have people coming up just wanting to meet you, simply because you are so confident that you automatically make an impression in their minds as being somebody different. Imagine how it feels to exude an attractive energy, one that radiates out and attracts people to you.

Confident people appear more credible. Being confident will immediately turbocharge your success in your business and your relationships because you will come across as more credible. If someone asks you a question, you will look him or her straight in the eye, have confident physiology, and answer in an authoritative tone. It took a few blown real-estate deals for me to learn this lesson the hard way. After all, if you don't project that you believe in yourself, how are investors supposed to believe in you?

Confidence can make your dreams come true. Right now, as I write this book, I am actually dictating it into an audiocassette recorder on a beautiful Thursday afternoon in Oregon. I hear geese quacking in the background. There's a beautiful blue sky reflecting off a lovely pond. It's a puffy-clouds kind of day, where you just want to relax and enjoy yourself. It is because of using the techniques I'm prescribing that I am able to do so.

My Journey to Unstoppable Confidence

Now, before you think that I was always this confident, let me tell you my story. I share this miserable tale of shyness to let you know that no matter how shy or unconfident you are now, you can improve and become more confident.

My Shy Self

I had always been shy as a child and continued as a shy young adult. I had a small, select group of close friends my entire life, but I never found enough confidence to introduce myself to a stranger. This led to serious difficulties for me in dating and relating to women.

My friends and I excelled in school; it was our main focus. Yet in the back of my mind I knew I was missing out on something when all the other people in high school were going out on dates. I thought to myself that I must be different or that something must be wrong with me. Consequently, I found myself rationalizing that I could be a great Lothario if I chose to, but that my main area of concentration and excellence was school.

However, deep down, I secretly desired to trade places with some of the other kids, just to experience what it was like to go on a date—or even be comfortable with someone of the opposite sex. The more I thought about how much fun they were having hanging out and having normal teenage experiences, the worse I felt about myself. It was as if I lacked the ability to really connect with another person at a deep level.

Searching for a way to escape, I turned to studying even harder and burying myself in books. At that time, it was all I knew how to do. Now, in reflection, I can easily see that there were other choices available at all times. We always have options, and it's important to be able to recognize as many of them as possible and then naturally decide for ourselves which option suits us best.

In four years of high school, I went on exactly one date. Of course it wasn't me who initiated it. The girl approached me after class one day and asked me if I wanted to hang out with her one night. Smiling broadly and trying to contain my overwhelming enthusiasm at this incredible, unprecedented event, I gladly accepted.

Later in the week, she called me and we set the date for the following Friday. When that night came, she picked me up and we went to a fast-food restaurant nearby. All throughout dinner, the conversation was strained as she tried her best to pry me loose from my shy shell. Every time I began to come out of the shell, I automatically retreated back into it simply because of my dreadful habit of shyness. She did her absolute best to talk with me and have a good time. Still, I could tell she saw my shyness as an obstacle to getting to know each other. My saving grace was that I smiled a lot and reciprocated every question she asked me. The conversation went better as long as she did the talking.

After we finished dinner, she drove us up to a mountainous lookout point with a beautiful view of the city. It was a clear night with the stars illuminating the sky. She asked me for suggestions on what I wanted to do, but I was too shy to suggest anything for fear of rejection. I didn't really understand the meaning of this field trip. Only later did I learn from other high school friends that the place we went to was the designated make-out spot.

While I was able to maintain good eye contact with the young lady, sometimes there were pauses in the conversation that seemed like an eternity to me. And at these times, my internal dialogue came alive as if it were an annoying younger sibling whose life mission was to prevent me from enjoying myself. "Does she want me to kiss her? What if I have some gunk in my teeth? If I kiss her, how should I do it? Does she really like me? Is she bored with me? What should I say next? Why are we really here? What does it mean? What should I do next? Do I look at the stars outside the car with her? Should I hold her hand? My goodness, she sure is pretty. Is she noticing me turning red with embarrassment? How come I'm so darn shy? Do I want to kiss her? When should I do it?"

The internal dialogue continued on and on like that for the entire night. No wonder I could not hold a conversation with her. How could I when I was so busy having a conversation with myself? None of my attention was left over to talk with her. After an hour more of forced conversation, she finally dropped me off at home and offered a handshake in lieu of repeating one of our previous awkward episodes.

Through the high school gossip grapevine, I found out that the young woman had recently broken up with her long-term boyfriend and immediately called to ask me out. And I wondered if it was really a coincidence that we had gone to the restaurant where he worked. Was she hoping he'd be there? My ultimate conclusion was that she was just trying to make him jealous and have him find out about our "date," even though she did seem interested in me.

People thought my inaction and unwillingness to initiate activities with others was because I was antisocial, aloof, indecisive, reactive, and generally unfriendly. What I found most painful was that I wanted to be social, proactive, decisive, and friendly—only at that time I did not know how. That was the most frustrating part, behaving as if I were trapped in a shell and unable to be who I really was all along.

My College Years

Now, as you've read about my ultrashyness in high school, you may be thinking that it couldn't get any worse. It did. Since I was so good at being shy, I really outdid myself in college. The more the years passed, the more I found my inability to be confident a glaring weakness.

My roommates meant well when they would try to get me to drink to loosen up. Their hearts were in the right spot, God bless them! They knew I was "stiff" and very shy. Instead of hanging out with them and drinking and socializing, I would while away my time on the computer, chatting with strangers through e-mail. How could I turn down the opportunity to hang out with my friends and instead chat with strangers halfway around the world? I rationalized it by saying I did not hang out with my roommates because I didn't drink. I didn't know I could still socialize with them if I was not drinking. That option, easily the most obvious choice now, never even crossed my mind.

One night, after a few too many beers, my roommates and their friends spotted me screwing around on the computer and decided to get me to loosen up. Their mission henceforth was to get me drunk as a skunk. They proceeded to apply some very persuasive peer pressure, inviting me upstairs where a party was being held. Being flattered that they even recognized me, I finally said yes and resolutely stated that I would not drink, though.

After getting upstairs and getting into the midst of the party, one of my generous roommates handed me an "orange juice" and said to drink up. In a state of gratitude for all the attention, I chugged it. The next thing I knew, I was feeling tipsy and really relaxed. My lips wouldn't stop moving, and I was having lots more fun. Through what I eventually realized was a semidrunken stupor, I figured out that the orange juice was spiked with alcohol. However, I was finally feeling accepted, so I chose to drink some more. It was my first experience with alcohol. And I found that I quite liked being able to drink to the point of obvious inebriation, since it allowed me to relax and stop being shy temporarily.

After that great first drinking experience, I decided I liked it and did it a lot more. When the weekend came, I talked to a number of people to find out where the party was being held. Once at the party, I proceeded to get seriously drunk. My faulty logic was that if one beer was good, then two beers would be even better. By following this logic, I was drunk in no time. And simultaneously, I transformed myself from a shy wallflower who spoke to no one into a raving, whirling dervish of a humorous drunk who spoke to people, told jokes, laughed loud and long, and had a great time.

It was at these parties that my friends had to tell me it was time to go home, but I never wanted to leave. This was my escape from my shy self, and I wanted it to last as long as possible. I needed it to last as long as I could make it. That was why I would metaphorically play the doctor, prescribing alcohol to myself as a self-medication for my shyness.

At this point in time, you may be wondering whether one of the *Unstoppable Confidence* techniques is to get sloshed and drown out your shyness with alcohol. The answer is no. It's just that at that time, I didn't realize there were other ways to overcome shyness.

As a result of these parties, I woke up in strange places, forgot what I had done the previous night when I was drunk, and felt miserable with a hangover. Still, in my mind, drinking was my ticket out of shyness. What I hadn't realized was that I had other options. But without these other options to be more confident, I did the best I could with what I knew. And that, unfortunately, was to drink to excess.

One day after having a miserable hangover, I crossed a threshold and knew it was time to stop. I decided that there had to be another way. After all, I had seen other people who behaved confidently without resorting to getting smashed. I decided I'd find out just what it was that they were doing.

My Search for Solutions

I began searching for answers. I found myself reading a number of self-help books. From each of these self-help books, I gained a little knowledge or a useful exercise to enhance my confidence in myself and allow me to relax in the presence of others. Finally, I promised myself that I would become confident in whatever I wanted to do.

I was fiercely determined to gain confidence. Ultimately, it was the experience of breaking out of my shell that made it possible. Specifically, in my case, it was talking to women. I decided that I would approach every single woman I saw! At first, I would simply smile at them. And you know what? They responded. Not all of them, but enough to encourage me to expand my comfort zone a little further.

This small success catapulted me to the next step in expanding my comfort zone. Next, I would approach women and simply say hi. Again, this slight widening of my comfort zone encouraged me. After all, I was an adult and had to take care of my confidence myself.

I had two choices. I could either retreat back to my comfort zone and be shy, blaming someone else for making me that way; or I could take responsibility and go for it. When my confidence really grew, I got to the point where I could meet women and gain instant rapport with them, conversing with them at ease.

Follow Your Dreams

Confidence ultimately gave me the ability to leave my job and start my own businesses. Confidence is what I needed to follow my dreams, and I'm sure that as you read this, you can find your own reasons why it's important for you to go out and find your own dreams. Picture your idea of bliss: What does it look like? What does it sound like? Who are you with? How much fun are you having? What time do you get up? What time do you go to sleep? Do you take a nap because you can?

No matter what your dreams are, when you use the techniques in this book, you'll develop the unstoppable confidence to go after those dreams and make them a reality. By keeping your vision in mind—imagining it vividly and regularly—you automatically teach your unconscious mind to lead you to that day. And won't that day be wonderful?

2

Origins of a Lack of Confidence

Courage is resistance to fear, mastery of fear—not absence of fear.

—Mark Twain

UP UNTIL NOW, HOW HAVE you thought of yourself? Were you shy, like I was? Were you tentative?

A lack of confidence usually comes from one of the following areas:

- Society at large
- Your parents
- School and your peers
- Mass media

In addition, you may have become shy because of hypersensivity, or even because you believe you were born that way.

In this chapter, we'll explore the reasons you may lack confidence. In the process, we'll debunk the false premises behind these reasons. If you have children, we'll discuss how you can prevent shyness from happening to them. You'll instill unstoppable confidence in them.

Society

In many ways, society conditions people to "go with the flow," to "accept what is offered," and not to "make any waves." Sometimes, this is falsely interpreted as advice to *not* follow your dreams. If you need to step outside of what is normal and usual to pursue your dreams, then do exactly that.

Parents

Parents can be major contributors to a lack of confidence. Throughout life, their purpose is to teach their children and help them to experience their full potential, to be who they were meant to be. Yet sometimes parents strip away the child's individuality and inadvertently instill what the child perceives as limitations. Parents often try to get kids to conform to the view of what they think is correct.

How many times have you heard the following phrases?

- "Act like a grown-up."
- "Stop acting childish" (as if that were a bad thing).
- "Be realistic."
- "Get your head out of the clouds."
- "You're such a dreamer."
- "You can't do that."
- "No one has ever done that before."

Parents usually have positive intentions motivating their behavior, yet sometimes they don't communicate that. Take the phrase "act like a grown-up." What does it mean? To have all the limits most adults do; to not play and experience pure joy like a child; to not learn, wonder, or explore? If that's acting like a grown-up, I'd rather pass.

Or consider the phrase "stop acting childish." The notion of exploring, laughing a lot, and learning a lot is really what life is all about, so it would seem that kids have the right idea after all. By this definition, "acting childish" is the natural state of humans.

What about the notion of "being realistic"? What does that really mean? Realistic according to whom? How specifically should I be realistic? The phrase is ludicrous. And calling people dreamers or telling them to "get your head out of the clouds" does not help them. It only instills limits in them and helps to bring them back into the bind of what is socially acceptable.

School

School has a huge influence over children. We're mandated to go. Teachers are powerful authority figures, and peer pressure is extremely high. We're all taught to fit in; everyone wants to fit in. So how does school create a lack of confidence?

One factor is peer pressure. Some kids make fun of anyone who does anything differently. School can also divide kids into different learning tracks, which is most unfortunate. Kids can be quite intelligent, much smarter than we typically give them credit for. They understand the labels that go with different learning tracks and they integrate these into their identities. The students labeled "slow" integrate this as a belief: "I stink at math." And these beliefs help shape their reality and their whole way of being.

A research study in the 1960s showed how powerfully expectation influences performance. One teacher was told her class of students was "exceptional," but in reality it was a standard cross-section of students. This "exceptional" class performed exceptionally that year, and the teacher commented on how eager the students were to learn and how much she enjoyed teaching them. The next year, another normal cross-section of students was in her class. This time, the experimenters told her that these students were poor performers. As expectation and beliefs create reality, the "poor" students performed awfully. The same teacher, who had just had the "exceptional" students the prior year, remarked how awful the students were, how much they hated learning, and how hard they were to teach.

We can take this same idea and project only positive expectations onto our own children. Furthermore, we can expect excellence from all the people we interact with. It will surprise you to learn how often people will rise up to whatever standards you set for them.

Mass Media

A lack of confidence can also come from the media. Mainstream media is funded by advertising, and ultimately it is out to get people to consume. Network television programming is free because advertisers give the networks large amounts of money in order to introduce their products to a captive audience. Terrestrial radio is free for the same reason. Individuality is dangerous to these advertisers because when you think for yourself, you can decide for yourself whether the product is right for you or not. You won't be buying for the sake of conformity and "keeping up with the Joneses."

It is to the advertisers' benefit if you lack confidence. They use tactics such as telling you that everyone else has the product and therefore you must need it as well. They teach you to feel bad if you don't have their products. They teach you that life can become an instant party if you consume their products.

My favorite example of this is the stereotypical beer commercial. You watch a less-than-healthy guy watching TV endlessly and see him given a beer. You already know what happens next, at least according to the commercial: life instantly becomes a party, beautiful women swoon over him, and he realizes he has his dream sports car, he is vacationing on a tropical island, and he can forget about any of life's ordinary troubles. It behooves the media to do this to sell more products.

Hypersensitivity

Sometimes being overly sensitive can lead to shyness. People can become afraid of doing anything for fear of offending someone or getting in trouble. Being supersensitive may be useful in some contexts, such as when you want to really empathize with another person, but if a person is supersensitive all the time then it becomes detrimental.

I know this because I used to be hypersensitive. I never spoke up, never stepped outside my comfort zone, and never did anything that might have the remotest possibility of aggravating people. This occurred as a result of my incapacitating fear. I figured that since I was so sensitive, others must be the same way. Therefore, I decided it was necessary to tiptoe around people so as to manage their feelings. Only later did I discover what nonsense this turned out to be.

It's important to be sensitive to a point, yet at the same time, you need to have confidence to do what it takes to achieve your goal. People are remarkably resilient. If you have confidence and accidentally hurt someone's feelings, there's a very simple remedy. You apologize, resolve not to do that again, and move on. It's really very simple.

The Myth of the Shy Gene

Some people label themselves as having a "shy gene," which brings me to the myth of genetic shyness. Many people simply accept their shyness and rationalize it by saying, "That's just the way I am." What a loaded phrase. These people need to stop saying that. It's as if they are chanting a negatively reinforcing mantra. The real secret is that it's a broken affirmation that keeps people stuck.

The affirmation "Every day and in every way I'm getting better and better" is a famous affirmation by Emile Coue, an early self-help pioneer. "I'm shy because that's the way I am" also works as an affirmation, but it should be appended with the statement "according to me."

You can decide that you were born with shyness, sure, but you can also decide to break free from it. The myth that a person simply is or is not shy is one of the worst myths ever passed on from disempowered people to other disempowered people. Believing that your parents were shy, which caused you to be shy, is no excuse. The same goes for your kids. People do not become shy automatically when they are born. There is no "shyness gene."

People become shy because they've learned to behave and act in a certain way. When I was shy around people, it was

because I was in the habit of looking at a person and thinking, "He (or she) won't like me." This thought always left
me feeling bad inside, picturing the person rejecting me,
and then feeling an immense and paralyzing fear. That was
simply the way I learned to behave. I only knew one way of
behaving, but fortunately I found more choices.

Your parents may or may not have influenced you to be
shy, but that's different from them inflicting you with some
untreatable genetic disease, which is really what it means
when people say, "That's just the way I am."

The Truth About Shyness

Let me tell you about the myth of "I'm shy." It's an excuse
that enables people to stay stuck. Shy is not a trait; it's only
a way of acting. If you can act one way, that means you can
act another way too. Shy is a behavioral mode; it's not an
adjective that describes a person.

It's not a state of being. It's a way of acting. You can
behave in a confident manner too. You always have that
choice. People locked into the "I'm shy" excuse don't realize
they have the choice.

Consider this: if you could choose your identity, if you
could choose the way you see yourself, then would you
deliberately label yourself as shy? As a person lacking confidence? As hesitant or anything less than glorious? Absolutely
not. And yet, that's unfortunately what so many people do
when they say "I'm shy," or "I'm just not confident," or anything else of that nature. Therefore, it's important to avoid
the phrase "I'm shy."

Worse than saying "I'm shy," though, is talking about
shyness as if it's some sort of disease or disorder. "Yeah, he
has a case of shyness." "She has shyness disorder." That is

the most ridiculous thing ever. If I walk into a room of shy people and a bug that's flying around bites me, do I become shy too? No. That is downright absurd. People don't go walking along one day and go "Ugh!" and crumple to the ground, and then get diagnosed with shyness.

Fear and F.E.A.R.

Have you ever watched kids play? They really know how to dig in and thoroughly enjoy themselves. When they're having a good time, kids totally embrace whatever they are doing at the moment with joyful abandon. Kids are true dreamers.

Children, in essence, have not been trained to see their own limitations the way adults have. In fact, children enter this world with only two natural fears:

- The fear of falling
- The fear of loud noises

Aside from these, all other fears are learned. Human beings are magnificent at learning. Because you have learned to fear other things aside from the only two natural fears, you can naturally empower yourself to move past your fear by learning new ways of behaving.

A study was conducted among adults to research their greatest fears, and the fear of public speaking rated higher than the fear of death. This is irrational! Being more afraid of public speaking than of death is a direct result of learning to fear something that does not need to be feared. Fear can be characterized by the acronym F.E.A.R., meaning False Evidence Appearing Real. When people realize that public speaking is simply a process and not a life-or-death event, the false evidence disappears and with it goes the fear. With the fear gone, people can be their naturally confident selves.

Confidence as Our Natural State of Being

A state of confidence should be our natural state of being. The fact is that when we're born, we are simply not self-conscious. It's not like we pop out of the womb and say, "Oh, I'm naked. Could somebody please get me some clothes here? Ooh, I'm shy now! Oh no, everybody's looking at me and I'm naked!"

Children are already in their natural state of being: absolutely confident, full of wonder, and ready to explore the world around them. What if we were to adopt that same childlike attitude for going after what we wanted in the world?

When you were first born, did you immediately stand up and start walking around as though it were completely normal to you? Obviously you did not. Neither did I, and neither did anyone else. In learning how to walk, children take the attitude, "Hey, I'm going to do this walking thing. I see others around me doing it and I know I can do it too. I'm going to persevere. It doesn't matter how many times I fall down. It only matters that I keep getting up." If you get the chance, watch kids as they begin to walk. They crawl around, stand up, wobble around, fall down, and then do it all over again. Kids continue doing this until they learn how to consistently walk. Nothing will stop them from learning how to walk. When you have this same attitude in going after your goals, nothing will stop you from achieving them.

What if kids were infected with the same useless attitudes that some adults have? "If we try something and it doesn't work, we just give up." We'd have all these people who refuse to walk just because they didn't get it down perfectly when they were kids. They tried it once and it didn't work, so they gave up. They decided they weren't walkers. Can you picture a little baby with his arms crossed, pouting, scowling intensely just because he took the lackadaisical adult attitude that if something doesn't immediately work then it's time to give up? Can you imagine a little baby saying in a snooty manner, "Walking isn't for me! I do other things. I've tried it once and it's really not all that it's cut out to be." Fortunately, kids keep on going and going until they master the skills. We as adults can learn from them and keep the same attitudes that children have toward learning.

3

What Is Confidence?

All our dreams can come true, if we have the courage to pursue them.

—Walt Disney

IN ORDER TO UNDERSTAND WHAT confidence is, it's necessary to define both what it is and what it is *not*. Once we are on the same page as to what confidence is and isn't, we can move forward toward gaining unstoppable confidence.

What Confidence Is Not

Confidence means many different things to many different people. Similarly, confidence also evokes certain feelings and automatic reactions within people. Before we go any further in shedding light on what confidence is, we will discover what it absolutely is not.

Arrogance vs. Confidence

Sometimes arrogance is mistaken for confidence. They're not the same things, folks. Arrogance is either a honed reaction or an affectation, but whatever it is, it's definitely something completely different from confidence. Arrogance leans toward elitism, being macho, showing off, and so on.

Have you ever seen those really huge guys with bulging muscles, the ones who are overdeveloped to the point that they find it necessary to thrust their chests way out and swagger in the utmost cocky way? This is an example of arrogance, not true confidence. It's as if they consider themselves better than everyone else solely because they're so large. True confidence comes from within—and when you realize *you* are confident, you do not feel the need to proclaim it to the world.

Now contrast the example of arrogance with the following example of true confidence. Stop for a moment and consider the famous, muscular movie stars Arnold Schwarzenegger and Sylvester Stallone. These guys do not go around with puffed-up chests, thinking they're better than everyone else. Instead, they have a quiet but powerful confidence that comes from an acute awareness of their abilities. This is a major difference, and we'll explore this further later in the book.

It is never necessary to shout from the mountaintops in order to convey that you are a confident individual. The people who do so are hardly ever as confident as they try to appear. I have met many people who are confident and many people who lacked confidence. The truly confident people all had a similar trait: their confidence came from within and it did not have to be voiced. A nonchalant, matter-of-fact confidence is ideal.

There is no need to brag about one's accomplishments. Those who brag are only masking their insecurity about themselves. Allow your results to speak for themselves. Actions speak louder than words, so take your confidence and make it happen.

If someone has to continually broadcast his or her "confidence," it really makes me wonder. It seems that this person is not really that confident at all; instead, the person is often trying to convince himself or herself by proclaiming it to others. In his or her own mind, this helps make it official. But the person is trying to gain confidence in an ineffective manner.

Confidence comes from within. And when you believe in yourself, others will believe in you too. This is a universal law and a secret known to all leaders. It does not work the other way around, no matter how much we would prefer it to. There are far easier and more effective ways to skyrocket your confidence than waiting for others to believe in you; you will learn them later on in this book.

Belligerence vs. Confidence

Now let's talk about the difference between belligerence and confidence, using relationships as an example. Sometimes, women are apparently attracted to jerks. I'm sure that many of us have seen examples of this in our lives, or perhaps know someone who is currently in this situation. On the surface, the jerk exhibits some "bad boy" traits that some women may perceive as confidence. The jerk has probably convinced himself that he has it all going on. What masquerades as confidence in the jerk is just belligerence, which presents itself in the form of a superaggressive attitude. You can and should always assert yourself whenever you deem it necessary. However, this does not mean bullying people, treating them badly, and trampling over them.

Belligerence is what makes a jerk just that. The jerk is abrasive and cares little for the relationships he forms with others; instead he chooses to bulldoze his way through life. True confidence, however, allows you to go through life easily, to efficiently get the results you want, and to make people feel good when you deal with them. Make people feel good even if it's for no other reason than just because you can.

True Confidence Comes from Within

Take a moment and think of an area of your life where you may be confident. Ask yourself this question: "How do you know that you are proficient at [name your area]?" And being completely honest with yourself, supply an answer. If you absolutely know that you are proficient in the area you chose because your own thought or feeling or belief system told you so, congratulations! You are really confident in that area. If you were not sure about your proficiency in your area or if you had to rely on external confirmation from your peers, spouse, or supervisor, you are not quite yet as confident as you can be. By the end of the book, after doing the exercises, you will be right there. When you have done all the exercises and completed this book, you will have the true confidence that comes from within.

Confidence—or a lack thereof—is a reality across all demographics. Across all races, all economic levels, all religions, there will always be some people who are confident and some people who are not. Even a rich and famous movie star, who many people envy and consider to "have it all," gets nervous at times because he or she wants to perform well.

Competence vs. Confidence

Are confidence and competence the same thing? No! In fact, they are quite distinct, and understanding the difference is essential. Competence is defined as the ability to do something, and confidence is defined as your belief about your competence. Each of us has individual experiences, beliefs, and values that make us perceive life in our own individual way. Everyone has his or her own perception of reality, a unique model of the world. This means that it is only a perception and not reality. The empowering part of this idea is that these beliefs can be changed and, in turn, change one's perception of life. This means that the exercises and strategies described in this book will change your beliefs and your perception of what is possible for yourself.

Confidence Without Competence

It is an absolute recipe for disaster to lack competence yet possess and project unjustified confidence. Take, for example, someone who has never flown a plane before but has ridden on a plane and thinks he is now an ace pilot, since he read a book once on it a decade ago. Would you let that person fly you across the country? I would get off that plane so fast that people would think I was a blur. You can easily see how there are numerous examples of confidence without competence—and why it's dangerous.

Competence Without Confidence

People who are competent and yet lacking in confidence are stuck in a quagmire. They might have a perfect understanding of some powerful concepts without ever taking action.

Someone who has the knowledge and competence to do something, and does nothing instead, is no better off than someone who is clueless and incompetent.

When I was getting started in real-estate investment, I was the classic example of competence without confidence. I studied, studied, and studied real estate. I read ten books, took three home-study courses, attended a seminar, and signed up for two mentoring programs. Still, I was stuck big time in a quagmire that I wasn't even aware one could get caught in. I saw others being successful and knew exactly what they were doing and how they were doing it. When I asked them about it, they confirmed to me that they were doing exactly what I was only thinking about.

What was holding me back? It was my lack of confidence and my fear of the unknown. I would've had to know absolutely everything about all of real estate before taking any action at all! So I kept studying and studying, trying in vain to learn everything so I could actually get started. Meanwhile, the people around me had their businesses taking off because they were taking action.

The Four Levels of Competence

There are four different levels of competence that people go through as they develop any skill. Those four levels are: unconscious incompetence, conscious incompetence, conscious competence, and unconscious competence. You will travel through these stages as you reach unstoppable confidence.

Unconscious Incompetence

Unconscious incompetence means you do not possess a skill, nor are you even aware of how useful that skill could be.

Someone who is extremely shy—and does not even rec-ognize how beneficial learning how to be more confident would be to him or her—could be considered unconsciously incompetent in the area of confidence.

I spent the first twenty years of my life like this. Being shy, I knew no other way of being nor was I cognizant of the fact that other people didn't have to live trapped in shy shells. By reading this book, you have already passed through this stage of unconscious incompetence. Picking up this book means you are looking for a better way to live, which means you're at least at the next stage (or perhaps further) on your unstoppable-confidence journey.

Conscious Incompetence

When I was in college, I finally looked around and realized just how shy I was and that other people were actually con-fident. I had moved to the second level of skill development, which is that of conscious incompetence. I became aware of just how shy I was. When we become aware of something lacking in our lives, that is a great opportunity because it means we get a chance to improve our lives. When I became conscious of my incompetence, I began reading numerous self-help books and doing exercises. I attended seminars, watched videos, and basically tried anything to further my confidence. The more I worked on myself, in the same way that you are doing now by reading this book, the further I moved toward conscious competence.

Conscious Competence

Conscious competence is a state of being in which you can apply a skill and yet you have to consciously think about applying the skill. The skill is not yet a habit for you. The vast majority of you at this point in the book are probably consciously unstoppably confident. You know how to be confident, and now it's a matter of developing this into a habit. Give yourself the gift of your own twenty-one-day unstoppable-confidence challenge. Deliberately practice your confidence for twenty-one consecutive days until you reach the skill level of unconscious competence.

Unconscious Competence

The fourth level of skill development is called unconscious competence. This is the ultimate stage of any skill. Unconscious competence is the state at which a skill has been ingrained as a habit. You no longer have to spend your time thinking about applying the skill. People who are masters at what they do function at the level of unconscious competence. If someone were to inquire about how specifically they perform at such high levels, they might not be able to verbally describe what they do. The reason for this is that they are no longer conscious of what they do in order to perform such great feats.

Competence Plus Confidence Equals Success

Being unstoppable means having both the competence and the confidence and going for it. This is what this book is all about: when you have the competence to do what you want and the confidence to follow through and take action, you are unstoppable!

4

The Nine Factors of Unstoppable Confidence

Courage is the first of human qualities because it is the quality which guarantees all others.

—Winston Churchill

NOW THAT WE'VE DEFINED WHAT confidence is and isn't, let's look at the nine factors that stand between you and unstoppable confidence. You must learn and memorize all of them if you wish to master this program and make your dreams come true. The nine factors are as follows:

- Experience
- Perception
- Decisiveness
- Empowerment
- Goals
- Action

- Motivation
- Momentum
- Commitment

Factor One: Experience

There are certain beliefs that are more empowering than others when you are doing something for the first time. How you perform the first time you take on a new challenge will affect how you perform when faced with it again later. Believing the following affirmations will enable you to achieve greater results more quickly.

There's a First Time for Everything

When doing something for the first time, remember:

- The first time I do this is the hardest.
- Each and every time I do this, it gets easier.
- When I succeed, I will study my actions so I can improve even more.
- If I don't get the right outcome, I'll learn from my mistakes and do things differently next time.
- It does get easier.

Keep these affirmations in mind as you overcome difficult tasks and tackle adversity in the form of something you have not done before.

The Confidence/Success Cycle

In this book, I've given you many generalizations about confidence. It's important, though, to define what confidence means to you specifically. What do you expect to see, hear, and feel when you experience confidence?

The reason it's important to know is so that when you achieve the level of confidence you desire, you will know that you have arrived.

With ultimate confidence in yourself, other people will believe in you too. Also, your belief in yourself will increase exponentially as others come to count on you. You will have the confidence to risk stepping outside your comfort zone, and you will find yourself achieving things that were previously impossible. This, in turn, will give you more confidence, and others will believe in you even further. This concept is the basis for the confidence/success cycle. Your confidence and success increase cyclically as you continue to push the limits and achieve like you never have before.

Factor Two: Perception

In the course of this book, I've introduced you to a lot of new concepts—some of which you've probably accepted straightaway, and others that you've no doubt had to think about more. I'll continue to give you new concepts and ideas that may challenge your old way of thinking. For instance, you may not believe this next concept—a key concept of neurolinguistic programming (NLP), described in more detail in the Introduction—at first, but as you think about it carefully you'll realize how pervasively it applies to your life already. Are you ready?

What Does It Mean?

Meaning does not exist as a concrete reality; it is purely a subjective phenomenon of perception.

How you think about something is entirely up to you. You can put a positive or negative frame around whatever experience you have in life. Since you always have a choice to either laugh or cry based on the experience, do whichever you prefer. I prefer laughing, so I find myself doing that more often.

A friend of mine told me this story. He was sitting on a bench in a park, right next to a rather large crack in the sidewalk. A man came by, tripped on the crack, and fell face-first into the bushes next to the sidewalk. Dusting himself off, he quickly got up and glanced around to see if anyone was watching. Unfortunately for him, my friend was watching the entire episode. Noticing this, the man turned several shades of red before hurrying away as fast as he could.

Later that same night, a woman came walking along the same path. At the same place in the sidewalk, she tripped and fell flat on her back. Her spontaneous reaction was to let loose with a full belly laugh. She laughed so hard she began crying. She acted as if the slip was the funniest experience ever, and it seemed she could not stop herself from laughing. By the time her laughter had died down, my friend was staring at her. Nonchalantly, she picked herself up, smiled and acknowledged my friend, and happily darted off into the night.

The meaning of any experience, event, or interaction can vary widely between two people because it's their choice as to what they make of it. If someone offers you an insult, remember that it's only that person's opinion. By adopting this useful belief, you can move through the world more prepared to deal with anything life throws at you. Contrast this with the way some people take insults personally and waste their valuable time and energy being bothered by them. You are a meaning maker, and if you perceive some comment to be derogatory, stop yourself and give it a more positive spin.

Do this because you can. Remember, nobody else has the power to determine your own perception of events— only you!

In my own life, I had a business project that went sour. For a while, I spent my time being bitter and frustrated, stuck in a victim mentality. Finally, I started to ask myself questions like: "What can I learn from this experience? What does the outcome of this project really mean?" When I asked myself these questions, I immediately recognized that I had shifted into a more useful mentality. What had been a sore point for me became an opportunity to look at the adversity as a challenge. It was now up to me to rise above and conquer a difficult situation in order to achieve the right outcome.

That is exactly what happened. Had I latched onto that victim mentality and refused to let go, I never would have completed my business project. Any time you choose, you can change your perception and create a new meaning for something.

Factor Three: Decisiveness

It's easy to identify people who have unstoppable confidence just by watching the way that they make decisions.

The Deciding Factor

Confident people make decisions rapidly and with a sense of finality. Once a decision is made, they are committed to it. They rarely change their minds. Confident people never waver because they know what they want.

As we saw earlier in the book, it is imperative to know what you want beforehand. That way, when either an opportunity or a problem presents itself, you can think hard and ask yourself, "Hey, is this congruent with what I want? Does this coincide with my personal policies and my integrity?" Asking yourself these questions allows you to size up the decision you are making so that you can come back with a decisive, confident answer.

The Steps of Confident Decision Making

Prior to undertaking anything, there are some things you have to know about yourself. This may sound simple enough, but it is sometimes very difficult to know what is in your heart.

- What is it that you want? What is your ultimate goal?
- What are the personal policies that influence your integrity?
- Who are you? What is it you stand for?
- What are the acceptable and unacceptable outcomes for your goal?

Asking yourself these questions when faced with any kind of decision will help you with confident decision making.

Before anything else, you need to take an inventory of yourself. Get to know yourself: who you are, what you stand for, where you are going, and how you are going to get there. When you know the answers, everything else becomes very simple.

Now, if a question, a problem, or an opportunity arises, you need to size up the situation from all angles in order to be a confident decision maker. Look at it from your position.

Look at it from the other side. Look at how your position will affect you over time:

- If you were to say yes to this decision and move forward with it, how would it impact your life?
- Imagine yourself a few months down the road after having said yes to this decision. Imagine one year. Five years. How is your life?
- Think about how the future might be if you said no. What might your life be like then? What might it be like a few weeks from now? A few months? A few years?

Once you see that picture clearly in your mind, decide if it's congruent with your goals. Let your goals be your road map.

Trust Your Internal Voice

Another difference between people who have unstoppable confidence and those who do not is that people with unstoppable confidence trust in their internal voices. Although they listen to others for feedback, they tend to rely more and place more weight on their own internal voice than the voices of those around them.

People who lack unstoppable confidence tend to listen to the voices of those around them far too much. This leads to a propensity for conformist thinking, because people listening to and following everyone else will naturally *become* like everyone else. People who are unstoppable have to rely on their internal voice. Otherwise they would allow everyone else with "stinking thinking" to convince them that whatever goals they are seeking to accomplish cannot be achieved.

Listening to your internal voice means that you recognize what is valid, useful feedback and what is negative, destructive criticism. People who listen to their internal voice are said to have an internal frame of reference. People who follow the voices of others are said to have an external frame of reference.

Internal and External Frames of Reference

The way to discover your personal style in this matter, if you haven't already, is to ask yourself the following questions:

- If nobody told you, would you know what to do?
- How do you know you've done a great job?
- Does someone else need to give you answers?
- Who decides if you're getting the best use out of your time?

As you answer each of these questions honestly, you might notice a pattern emerging. If your answers are based on others' feedback, right now you have an external frame of reference. If your answers are based on your internal voice or your gut feeling, you have an internal frame of reference.

Factor Four: Empowerment

When you are unstoppably confident, there is a powerful difference between you and the "normal" population. The difference is control. You have more control over your environment, over your emotional state, over your beliefs, and ultimately over your actions. That is the simple difference between people who are empowered and people who are not. People who are not empowered have excuses.

Control

People who are not empowered have all the reasons why it is impossible to be, do, or have something. Those who are unstoppable realize that everything they want to do is under their own control. They are the masters of their own universe. If they don't know how to do something, they realize that there's some other resource that will teach them how to do it.

I like to think of myself as a "reverse paranoid." A reverse paranoid is a person who thinks that the universe is perfect and that everybody on the planet wants to help him or her achieve his or her dreams.

By the law of reciprocity, in order to fulfill my dreams I'm going to help others make their dreams come true. The universe works for and rewards those who serve others. The greater the energy that you put forth, coupled with the service you provide to others, the better the results you will enjoy. When you ask yourself, "How can I be of service to others today?" you will experience a paradigm shift of great proportions.

Greater Empowerment Equals More Choices

Empowered people simply have more choices than disempowered people. People who do not allow themselves to find other choices available to them are likely to become disempowered. Always contemplate the number of choices you have in any given situation and do your best to generate more options. Perhaps there is an option you have not thought of that would be ideal.

All you need to do now to empower yourself is to think of a solution and then act on it. With greater empowerment comes a truer sense of freedom because you have the liberty to choose from more options.

Adding More Options to Your Life

There's an easy way to add more options to your life. Pay attention to how people use language. Language indicates how we view the world, and it can either empower us or limit us through what we say. Some people use their language to try to force limitations on you.

Any time someone offers you only two choices, beware. Ask yourself if there are any other choices that have not been mentioned. Is there anything stopping you from choosing both options? The more options you have the more empowered you are, which means you will have a greater chance of success.

Salespeople are taught to intentionally use their language to limit our apparent choices. For example, let's suppose you've found a certain model of automobile you like. The salesperson might say something to the effect of: "Now that you've decided on this car, would you like to pay with cash or do you want to finance it through us?" This question automatically assumes that you are going to purchase the car, with the only remaining detail being how, specifically, you want to pay for it. Even if you did want to purchase the car, there might be another payment option that the salesperson's limiting statement hasn't covered. What if there were a hybrid part-cash, part-financing option? That is not reflected in the salesperson's statement.

Here are some questions to generate more options when you are presented with only a few:

- What's stopping us from doing both (or all) the options?
- What other options haven't we examined yet?
- Are these our only options?

Disempowered people simply find themselves to be lacking choices and are thus compelled to act upon their addictions—not out of choice but out of sheer necessity. Even if we were to consider psychopathic criminals, they appear as if they are "forced" to perform their evil deeds. In interviews, they often reveal how they went to great lengths to cover up what they did because they internally understood that it was wrong. Inevitably, the question gets posed to them of why they perpetrated the violent acts, if they truly understood the acts were immoral and wrong. They acknowledge that while they knew it was wrong, they felt as if they had no other options and their criminal acts were their only choice. Again, this is simply their perception of reality.

I am not condoning or apologizing for criminal behavior, but rather pointing out the fact that people need to make better choices for themselves, and to do that they first need to become aware of those choices and realize their validity.

The initial step to becoming more empowered is to eliminate the belief that you have few choices and replace that belief with the knowledge that you have many choices. You always have the freedom to choose. No matter what the situation, even in times where there is apparently a lack of choice, there really is a solution. When you keep this belief as you go through life, you will find you have an enriched sense of control over your life, which escapes most people.

Factor Five: Goals

A natural complement to unstoppable confidence is being goal-oriented. Goal orientation and confidence form a combination that will make all of your dreams come true.

Set Some Goals

Have the foresight to know what you want out of your life. Set up your long-term goals so that when they are fully realized, you will find yourself living your dream. With your long-term vision defined, plan out your medium-range goals. These are the goals that are in between your immediate, short-term ones and your long-term vision. When you accomplish your medium-term goals, you will know you are on the right track to achieving everything you want.

Break down all of your medium-range goals into smaller, more immediate goals that you will accomplish in the next year. Then continue breaking down the goals until you have monthly and then weekly ones. Finally, you will have specific actions to undertake each and every day in order to move you ultimately toward your dream life.

Set an outcome for everything you do and live life with purpose. You will be glad that you did. The way a climber reaches the summit of a mountain is to continue putting one foot after another toward the top. It's the same way one runs a marathon: one step at a time. What is essential is to always keep going. Never quit. Do it now.

A Harvard study on goal setting took place in the 1950s, and there was a follow-up study in the 1980s. The study in the 1950s showed that only 3 percent of the respondents had set goals at the time of their graduation. By the 1980s, this 3 percent was financially worth more than the remaining 97 percent combined. These people had focus and direction, and these were displayed by the setting of their goals. To gain the maximum benefit from this book, we will begin this journey we are taking together by setting goals: your own personal goals.

Outcomes vs. Goals

Outcomes and goals are similar in scope, but they have subtle differences. Goals typically have weightier stakes attached, whereas an outcome is a mini-goal that you desire from a particular situation. A goal is a dream with a deadline.

When I hang out with my friends, the outcome I want is simply for us to have a good time. I don't have a goal when I'm hanging out with them. My most recent goal in life is to sell a certain number of copies of this book within the next year. The magnitude of this goal and this outcome differ.

Though outcomes are much smaller in scope, they are still very useful. By identifying what you want out of any activity or interaction, you will be much more likely to obtain it. If I didn't know what I wanted out of an interaction or activity, how would I know how to proceed? I wouldn't!

After you decide on your outcome or goal, figure out what it's going to take to accomplish it. What kind of person will you have to be in order to make your dreams come true? Once you know, commit to becoming that kind of person.

Smart Questions for Making S.M.A.R.T. Goals

Stop for a moment and answer these questions:

- What do you want to get out of this book?
- What's stopping you from getting this right now?
- What's important to you about achieving your goals?

- What will it be like for you to have unstoppable confidence?
- What will having unstoppable confidence do for you?
- Are you ready to eliminate all your fear, uncertainty, hesitation, and doubt forever?
- How will you know when you have unstoppable confidence?

After answering these questions, you are now ready to set a S.M.A.R.T. goal for yourself. The acronym S.M.A.R.T. stands for:

Specific
Measurable
Achievable
Realistic
Timed

Specific. You make an outcome specific when you state what you will see, hear, feel, and experience. These will help to provide points you can check to verify that you have undoubtedly achieved your desired outcome. A general outcome might be: "I want to get confidence out of this book." That does not work as well as the following *specific* outcome: "I want to gain two specific strategies for eliminating my fear of changing jobs and gain confidence in knowing I will succeed at whatever job I have."

Measurable. Your outcome is measurable when you have a clear way to know whether you have met it or not. An immeasurable outcome is: "I will become confident by the end of the book from using the techniques described in its pages." While confidence is sometimes difficult to measure, you can get creative and find ways to do just that. A more measurable outcome is: "I will make more direct eye contact with people in my new job; I will maintain confident physiology, posture, and bearing; and I will be more outgoing by initiating conversations with my coworkers."

Achievable. Ensure that your outcome is achievable: that it is physically viable for you to accomplish. Ensure that you have a good likelihood of success. Remember that while you are unstoppable and you can achieve anything you desire, you must simultaneously plan a smooth progression, a driving movement from point A to point B that stretches your comfort zone as you march toward success.

Avoid setting yourself up for frustration by setting an outcome that is unattainable in a realistic time frame. Plan your progression; know the small steps along the way that will lead you to your ultimate goals. Set achievable goals, achieve them, and reset your goals even higher!

If you feel like the shyest person in the world right now, setting a goal to instantly be the life of the party will only set you up for a rude awakening. You can and will be the life of the party if you want, eventually, but first begin with these early steps, like talking to strangers and confidently asking about how they are doing.

Realistic. Realistic outcomes are outcomes that are, by definition, obtainable. If you want to grow wings and fly, that is not going to happen. Asking for an unrealistic outcome only sets you up for failure. When you set realistic outcomes, you will be proud of yourself when you achieve them.

Before Neil Armstrong landed on the moon, few people in America believed it was possible. However, a team of U.S. scientists knew that it would work in theory. To this end, they designed the Apollo missions that went to the moon, and the rest is history. As long as your outcome has a basis in reality or theoretical feasibility, it is realistic.

Timed. Make sure your outcome is timed by attaching a specific deadline to its accomplishment. I often ask people what their dreams are and as they start to glow with euphoria, they describe them to me in perfect detail. Later on in the conversation, I inevitably ask them what their goals are: immediate, short-term, and long-term. Their goals, if any, are radically different and do not bear any resemblance to their dreams. Their dreams are what they really want. Those dreams are unlikely to be achieved unless there is a deadline attached—along with a workable plan on how to achieve them.

Goals are dreams with deadlines. Impotent goals do nothing for one's motivation. That is why it is so important to have an outcome for this book and a timeline as to when you want to achieve your specific, measurable results. A good example is: "By the time I finish this book, after I gain unstoppable confidence, I will be able to walk up to any stranger and introduce myself." Another good example is: "I will feel calm and relaxed when talking to strangers in social situations."

Setting a Goal Contract

Along with all the other goals you are setting, I want you to set a goal for your confidence. I want you to set a specific, measurable, achievable goal for your confidence, and I want you to see it through to the finish. I've used this concept in the past for goals in all areas of my life, and I always find it to be amazingly effective.

Write out your goal, using all of the S.M.A.R.T. criteria that we have discussed, and at the bottom of the page, make a space for your signature, your name, and the date. At the top of this sheet, give it the title of "Goal Contract." The legal definition of a contract is a meeting of minds, so as you write out this contract and sign it, think of it as a meeting of your conscious and your unconscious minds. This becomes a "legally binding" document, a legal contract that you must execute because of its binding power. Whether it's asking someone out for a date or demanding a raise from your boss, I want you to make it a goal to assert yourself confidently in at least one area of your life by a certain date in the near future. Remember, you're under contract!

Factor Six: Action

Two young women both attended the same graduating class in college fifteen years ago. Samantha became a lawyer and Cathy worked as an engineer in the high-technology field. They both are proud parents with successful careers and faithful marriages. They own their own homes and by all appearances seem to lead happy lives. The only thing missing is a sense of fulfillment in their careers.

While they are both technically successful at their careers, they are equally disenchanted with them. Samantha does not find what she is doing fulfilling, and neither does Cathy. They used to eagerly look forward to work every day. Fifteen years later, however, something inside each of them has changed and they no longer find their careers rewarding. They both would rather pursue their true passions.

Samantha has always loved baking and wants to open her own bakery. She learned how to bake as a child and has always enjoyed it. Samantha knows that if she could own a bakery, it would be a smashing success. She envisions people coming from miles around to purchase her baked goods.

Cathy has always loved music. She grew up listening to music every spare moment she could and singing in her church choir. She currently sings in her women's group, yet she visualizes what it would be like for her to be a pop singer with her own CD, performing for vast audiences across the country.

Fast-forward five years. Samantha, while still yearning to open her bakery, has taken no action to actually make her dream come true. During each day that passes, she feels like she is wasting time at her job while she lives someone else's dream. Instead of jumping out of bed in the morning, she has to nag herself internally until she rolls out of bed and heads into work. She yearns for Fridays and absolutely despises Mondays. Spending the majority of her waking hours doing something she finds despicable, she feels as if she is wasting her life.

Cathy has taken tremendous action in the past five years and consequently has an album out, tours the region, and has the kind of fan response that creates sold-out shows. The ideal lifestyle that she dreamt of five years ago has manifested itself through her efforts. She cherishes each and every moment of her life. The time she spends on stage singing is the time when she feels that she is the most alive. She doesn't just *exist*; she knows she is living well. It seems as if her life gets better and better each and every day.

Sure, she has had her struggles in launching her own CD and getting her name to be recognized. She had countless people tell her no. In the face of defeat, she persisted. She never quit. It would have been easier to stay at her old job, and yet it would have been tremendously unfulfilling. Cathy paid the price through her commitment to live her dreams and she ultimately made them come true.

Samantha and Cathy both had dreams and visions for their respective futures. Cathy took action and fulfilled her dreams. Samantha did not. The difference between the two is that Cathy had the confidence to put her plan into motion by taking action. Samantha lacked the confidence. But the techniques Cathy practiced, combined with the attitudes and beliefs she and other successful people hold while they pursue their dreams—these can be learned and put into use. Most successful people may not be consciously aware of these techniques, but it's subliminally applied techniques like these that helps people like them achieve their intended results.

Put It into Action!

Confidence comes by finding out what—specifically—you want, making a plan to get it, and putting your plan into action! If you're doing well, ask yourself how it is that you're doing so well, and consequently you will know how to apply yourself and do even better. If you haven't been getting the results you want yet, evaluate what you are doing wrong, adjust your behavior accordingly, and do things differently.

As much as I'd like to say that all you have to do is incorporate these mental techniques into your life to get confidence, the truth is that unstoppable confidence comes from *doing*. These mental techniques will help you out, guaranteed. Yet the most confident people out there are confident because they have *proven* to themselves over and over again that they have reasons to be confident, because they have succeeded so many times. These people know in the deepest parts of their minds, bodies, and souls that they are capable doers.

The process of gaining confidence requires action. The goal contract you set in the preceding section isn't going to fulfill itself; you will need to *do* something. Only taking action can get you the undisputed, real confidence that you desire and deserve.

Factor Seven: Motivation

Another key to being a go-getter is how you motivate yourself. Do you motivate yourself with pleasure or with pain? Do you think about all the excellence you want in your life, or all the trouble you want to avoid? You motivate yourself in one of those ways—and only you know which one. Are you moving toward your goals or are you moving away from problems?

Methods of Motivation

Both strategies can be effective in certain contexts. For example, trial lawyers often use a pain-avoidance strategy in order to construct strong cases for their clients. They seek to minimize any damages that the opposing attorney might try to inflict by creating strong counterarguments.

The strategy of being pleasure-motivated can be equally effective. In fact, a majority of the most successful people who have close family relationships, massive financial success, and career satisfaction have motivation strategies drawing on the pleasure principle.

You may have already realized which motivation style you predominantly utilize. In having unstoppable confidence, I encourage you to focus mostly on having a positive motivation strategy, allowing you to seek better things in your life. The most successful people have the positive motivation, and if we want the same results then naturally we should follow suit.

The Value of Negative Motivation

While having a strategy to move toward excellence can be beneficial in certain circumstances, there are times when you can also benefit by having a strategy that moves you away from pain.

Since we all move toward pleasure or away from pain, we are always motivated to some degree by one or the other, and sometimes by both. Because I wanted to get this book done in a timely manner, not only did I commit myself to moving toward the pleasure of having the book published, but I also instituted a monetary fine on myself for not meeting my writing goals. After I began using this pain-avoidance motivation, my efforts skyrocketed and I became tremendously more productive. As you think about how I've applied this, you can begin to see all the ways in which you can utilize "toward pleasure" and "away from pain" motivation methods in your own life.

When you set up your "away from pain" strategy, make the negative incentive something more than slightly annoying, but not a catastrophe (just in case some unforeseeable event leaves you unable to achieve your outcome). Your strategies ought to be proportional to the magnitude of the goal you have set. Here's an example: if you're on a diet and you have a piece of cake, you obviously wouldn't punish yourself by fasting for the rest of the week. That would be ridiculous. You want your pleasure rewards and pain punishments to be commensurate with the goal. Instead, if you eat some chocolate cake while you're on a diet, you might figure out how many calories you ingested so that the next time you work out, you will burn that many extra calories beyond your normal workout.

Make It a Habit to Stay Motivated

Remember, people become addicted to various things all the time. Gambling, drugs, and alcohol are a few of the many destructive addictions people have. The secret is to aim our addictions in a positive direction. People who have unstoppable confidence have it because confidence is a positive habit of theirs. What makes the difference in our lives is the quality of the habits we form. Each of us has habits already; let's empower ourselves to have only positive, life-affirming habits and addictions.

Habits are tremendously powerful. Without them, there'd be so many decisions to make each day that we'd easily go on information overload (as if we weren't almost there already). Habits simplify our lives by making it so we don't always have to think about what to do; we just do it. That's why it's critical to develop good habits.

On your goal contract, make it one of your goals to develop the confidence habit. Make it another goal to pay attention as you become more and more confident; evaluate your progress.

Keep a Confidence Journal

I strongly recommend you keep a "confidence journal" so you can see just how far you've come. By the time you are fully aware that you have unstoppable confidence, you'll review your journal and naturally you'll be amazed to discover just how differently you think and feel. By regularly reviewing your journal, you'll also be able to immediately correct yourself so that you can have more confidence in the present and stay motivated toward your future goals. In your journal, feel free to jot down notes on what specific techniques from this book you will utilize in the next interaction to cause you to be even more confident.

Factor Eight: Momentum

Momentum is very valuable for increasing your confidence level. One of Newton's laws of physics states that an object at rest tends to stay at rest unless it is acted upon by an outside force. Similarly, an object in motion tends to stay in motion. Applying the same law to confidence shows that if you are at rest, it may be a bit difficult to begin increasing your confidence. However, after overcoming the initial resistance, the rate at which you gain confidence in yourself will soon accelerate. For people who have unstoppable confidence, it's even easier to accelerate the rate at which you gain confidence.

Stop for a moment and take a survey of how much momentum you have in your life. Are you in motion? Are you out there making it happen? Or are you going a little slower? Only you can honestly judge this for yourself. Do you need to crank it up a notch?

No matter where you are, you can always increase your momentum. The best way to do this is by starting small. As you continue to take small steps each and every day, you draw closer and closer to your goals. The small things add up, and pretty soon you will be leading the life of your dreams. After you're at the top of your mountain, having fulfilled all of your goals, you can look back at what you've done and marvel at how all those small actions you took led up to your massive success. These small actions can be any number of things; they can even be simple steps to educate yourself on the goal you've set your sights on (buying books, attending seminars, and so on).

The way I became a full-time real-estate investing entre-preneur was by subscribing to the aforementioned strategy. I learned a branch of real-estate investing called creative real-estate investing that requires neither money nor credit, because when I started I had neither! What I did to allow me to go full-time into the business was that I read a lot of books, attended a few seminars on real estate, made some offers on houses each week, and made calls to sellers after work every day.

Every day you are either moving toward your goals or away from them. Personally, I want to always be moving further toward them. Momentum is infinitely powerful and you can make it work for you or against you. Make it work *for* you!

Factor Nine: Commitment

When people commit themselves to their destiny, they go for it full-tilt and consequently achieve their goals. Master motivational speaker Anthony Robbins says, "Success is cut-ting off all of your options for failure."

As you realize what you specifically want out of life and decide that you're willing to pay the price to achieve it, you must be willing to commit yourself and cut off all options that lead to anything less than achieving your goal.

Commitment is very powerful in fulfilling your dreams. Many people say, "Don't burn your bridges." I'm just the opposite. I say, "Learn to burn, and burn very well!" Find out what you want to do, commit yourself to it 100 percent, and then burn away any options for failure. Ask yourself about all the excuses that might prevent you from accomplishing your goal. After you do that, go through and torch each bridge so that the only option is success, because you've committed yourself to that result.

When I left my corporate job as an engineer in a major semiconductor company, I committed myself mentally, emotionally, and spiritually to living the lifestyle of my dreams by burning all of my bridges. All of my ties to the company and potential for getting my job back instantly vanished as options. Even if I went back begging for a job, no job would be available to me. Success became the only option.

You can do the same thing with your goal. Decide what you want, commit to it, and systematically burn all the bridges that might stand in your way.

PART 2

Gaining Momentum

5

Confidence Is a Process

It's not what happens to you that determines how far you will go in life; it is how you handle what happens to you.

—Zig Ziglar

CONFIDENCE IS NOT A THING; it is a process. You may still be thinking of confidence as something that you either have or do not have, but that's not the case. Calling something "confidence" is actually a misnomer. There is only such a thing as acting confident or behaving in a confident way or thinking confident thoughts.

The same goes for any emotion, be it fear, sadness, depression, or anxiety. None of these are actual "things." They are the result of processes, sequences of thought that you run in your mind. Up until now, you may not have been aware that you were doing this, but the vital point to realize is that you have complete control over these processes. You can decide which mental processes are useful and which are not, and if they are useless, you can stop, interrupt, and banish them.

By Changing Your Language You Change Your Life

As we saw in the Introduction, neurolinguistic programming (NLP) shows how language, both verbal and nonverbal, affects our minds. The language you use to describe what you are feeling impacts your feelings tremendously. It is your knowledge and awareness of these processes that gives you power over them. When somebody says he or she is depressed, what that person has done is built that notion into his or her very being. People can't be depressed all the time; if they were, they wouldn't call it depression. It'd just be their normal state of being. Instead, people who consider themselves depressed should be saying, "I run a process through my mind that causes me to experience certain feelings that I have collectively labeled as depression." The same goes for anxiety.

Releasing the Past

Think about who you were in the past. Who cares if you were shy or if you weren't confident in the way you wanted to be? The past is behind you. There's nothing we can really do about it now; the best thing we can do is learn from it and behave differently in the future. To that end, I want you to forgive your former self for being shy and for not acting confident in the past. So often people spend their valuable time and energy kicking themselves for time and opportunities they lost as a consequence of being shy.

So stop now, before you read any further, and if you were unconfident or shy in the past, forgive yourself now. Release all those feelings of negativity and frustration, or anything bad you might have against your shy former self, because that version of you is over. We're going to learn from the past and we're going to move on!

Get Rid of Negative Emotions

Let's begin to blow out those negative emotions. A great place to interrupt and banish those useless thought processes is to consider the language you use to describe them. Let's say you've feared public speaking. How would you describe this fear? If you say, "I have a fear of speaking in public," you are, in a sense, taking ownership of something that is just a mental process!

What if you were to describe what is really happening and say, "When I think about speaking in public, I run a process in my mind that I have labeled as 'fear.'" How much does that change things for you? How much better do you feel, knowing that what you previously described as "a fear of public speaking" is really just a process that you can reverse?

Begin now to notice how you have been describing other negative emotions. Have you been saying things like, "I always get nervous when I talk to strangers," "Talking to customers makes me anxious," or "I just feel depressed"? Instead of saying "I feel sad," describe for yourself what is really going on: "I choose to think in a certain way that results in my feeling sad when I encounter a certain set of circumstances." It may sound a bit hokey at first, but as you continue to think about it and really dig into the meaning of that sentence, you will begin to gain a sense of how truly liberating this is.

Add Positive Emotions

Now, after taking control of these processes, insert a positive emotion in place of the negative one. "I have absolute con-

fidence in public speaking." Try that out. The negative processes do not serve you. If you catch yourself running one
of these negative processes, interrupt it. Inside your mind,
yell "*Stop!*"

Make it a habit to stop the negative process and automatically start the resourceful one. As you go through your day,
become aware of what you are seeing, hearing, and thinking
inside yourself and realize that you have control. Change
your physiology to reflect a confident state. Change your
internal voice to suit you.

Congratulate yourself when you stop the negative processes and praise yourself when you start a confident process, because you get more of what you reinforce. Praising
yourself gives you incentive to run the resourceful process.
Naturally, you'll then be more likely to do it again in the
future.

After all, you should treat yourself well. Some people
have negative internal voices nagging at them all day. How
awful would it be to live like that? Remember, the only
person with whom you spend all your time is yourself. You
might as well have great rapport with yourself. Also, don't
forget to congratulate yourself whenever you step outside
your comfort zone. Celebrate those successes and reward
yourself accordingly!

Consider the example of Janet, a rookie salesperson. Janet
finds herself saying, "Talking to customers is scary. They
frighten me and I feel fear when I go to ask them to purchase
my product. I just don't know what to do."

What is occurring here is that Janet has given up her personal power by using disempowering language. If we were
to reword her language in a way that would allow her to
easily change her perception of the situation, the translation
would be: "According to me, right now, talking to customers causes me to experience a certain emotion that I describe

as 'scary.' I choose to allow customers to frighten me, and I feel something that I label as fear when I ask them to purchase my product. I don't know what to do yet."

Here is what Janet can do to immediately gain control over her emotions:

• Append "according to me at this time" onto every one of her sentences. This forces her to acknowledge that what she is describing is not absolute truth and not etched in stone for all time.

• Whenever there is an unwanted emotion (like fear, guilt, or anxiety), she must describe the emotion with the following phrase: "I choose to experience a certain emotion by doing something inside my mind that causes me to experience a set of pictures, sounds, and feelings that I collectively have labeled [emotion]." This requires Janet to take the fixed emotion and turn it back into a process. It also demonstrates that she is the one in control of the process.

• When she catches herself using that disempowered language, after she restates it using the guidelines above, she must empower herself by using sentences that state how she will behave in the future. An example is: "Although I've done that in the past, I wonder how quickly I will find myself becoming more relaxed and confident when I go to ask the customers to purchase my product."

As you go through this example and see how it's done, you will realize you can do it too.

Unwanted Emotions Exercise

It's now time for you to think of five unwanted emotions and a context in which you experience those emotions. While you do that, become cognizant of the language you are using to describe what you really do to experience those unwanted emotions, and think of emotions that would best fit in their place after you rid yourself of the unwanted ones. Following that, do the exercise of changing your current language and adding in more empowered language.

Remember that when you change your language you change your life. Throughout the rest of this book, you'll be learning many more effective and simple ways to use language, and many more mental processes that will give you unstoppable confidence.

6

Your Beliefs and How They Affect You

If you develop the absolute sense of certainty that powerful beliefs provide, then you can get yourself to accomplish virtually anything, including those things that other people are certain are impossible.

—Anthony Robbins

THE NEXT STEP IS TO take a close, hard look at our beliefs, to find out what they really are—and what we really want out of life!

Your Current Beliefs Realized

Pause for a moment and consider everything around you. Everything that you have and everything that you lack stems directly from a belief of yours. Similarly, all of the experiences you've had and all of those experiences yet to be had are because of your beliefs. Beliefs are pervasive throughout all areas of our lives. They influence what we do and how we do it to an extraordinary degree. Your quality of life depends upon the quality of your beliefs; the more useful and empowering the beliefs you hold, the more success you will attract. Understanding why we have beliefs and—more importantly—how we can consciously change them is one of the key precepts of NLP.

Beliefs are very influential in our lives. They have the ability to spur us into action and fulfill our dreams or to keep us stuck in a mediocre situation. The difference that makes the difference is the quality of your beliefs. By observing a person's actions, you can deduce what beliefs he or she holds dear. If someone has a successful and happy relationship, you can deduce that he or she believes strongly in commitment to his or her partner. If someone has well-adjusted children, you can deduce that the parents believe in taking pride in being good parents. If someone is fit and muscular, you might guess that this person has a firm belief in health and fitness.

How Beliefs Are Formed

As we go through our lives, each of us gains a different set of experiences and learns to derive meaning from them. These lessons go a long way toward forming our beliefs. We acquire beliefs not only through our own experiences, though, but also through learning from the authority figures in our lives. These people have a way of passing on their beliefs to us.

Usually, when we are young children, the authority figures are our parents and schoolteachers. During this period, we do not consciously filter out what we don't want to believe or try to determine whether a belief is empowering to us. Since they are authority figures, we simply adopt their beliefs as if they were incontestable facts. This is useful, since there is so much for children to learn, yet sometimes those same well-meaning authority figures pass on less-than-beneficial beliefs. As adults, however, we should realize that there is a better way, which is to adopt beliefs based on their utility to us.

Ask yourself whether a particular belief serves you. If so, keep it. If the belief keeps you stuck in a station of your life that you've outgrown, get rid of it and replace it with a more empowering belief.

You can learn something from each and every person you encounter, whether it's something positive that you want to incorporate into your own life or something negative that you want to avoid. When you find that someone has empowering beliefs in a certain area, you can adopt those beliefs for yourself. Similarly, if someone tries to pass a limiting belief on to you, be sure to filter it out.

Consistently remain aware of your beliefs about certain things in different contexts—for example, you can wear a rubber band around your wrist and snap it every time you catch yourself uttering something less than empowering. This will cause your mind to associate that belief with pain, and since the mind wants to avoid pain at all costs, eventually it will eliminate that belief. Make it a habit to eliminate the beliefs that you notice tend to be useless or that are holding you back. Make it a habit to believe even more strongly in the empowering ones.

Sometimes people mislabel their feelings and create faulty beliefs. For example, if someone gets excited before making a sales pitch and mistakenly labels the feeling as fear, this person may create a belief that selling is always going to be scary. The next time he goes out to sell, it will be even harder for him to perform at his optimum level, since he believes he is about to get scared. That's a belief that should clearly be lost! Pay close attention to how you label your emotions, because that will determine whether you create useful beliefs or useless ones.

The Structure of Beliefs

Beliefs are structured in one of two ways: meaning or causality. When you hear either "meaning" or "causality" language (explained below), you know someone is sharing his or her beliefs with you. I personally find it useful to listen for signs of other people's beliefs in case they have a more empowering belief than one I currently hold. If they do, I know that I can replace my belief with theirs. Using the same idea, if I notice that they hold beliefs that I find less than useful to myself, I simply respect their beliefs and avoid adopting them as my own.

Meaning beliefs reveal what someone considers the definitive explanation of a given subject. *Causality beliefs* reveal what someone considers the definitive correlation between two subjects. Whenever you hear one of the following words, someone is exposing one of his or her beliefs:

- Means
- Is
- Causes
- Because

When you hear someone else's beliefs, it is important to realize that they are not necessarily true. Sometimes people forget that fact and accidentally take on less-than-empowering beliefs as their own. This is especially true for people listening to authority figures; they may forget to question what purpose is served by the beliefs the authority figure is trying to promote.

The Qualities of Beliefs

Beliefs have certain qualities that allow them to be encoded as beliefs in your mind. Each belief has certain visual, auditory, and emotional qualities associated with it (see the Appendix for a list of specific qualities). By altering any of these qualities, we alter the belief. By consciously directing our minds, we can deliberately manipulate these qualities in order to keep only the most empowering beliefs.

Visual Qualities of Experiences

Movie stars are often adored to the point that they are mobbed by fans and depicted as larger than life. The reason for this is because they are literally presented to audiences as larger than life on huge movie screens in theaters. In the same way, if you think about certain things as though you are viewing them on a mental movie screen, these things will seem quite compelling. If you have something positive that you want to experience more vividly, you can enlarge whatever you are visualizing—make it movie screen–size in your mind—and notice how that feeling becomes more intense.

You can make that belief even more intense by making it brighter in your mind and picturing it being closer; it's just like switching seats to move to the front row in a movie theater. When you visualize a belief or a memory as very bright and close, you will experience the feeling as much more intense. The reverse is also true. If you want to make something less powerful, you can visualize it as being small, dark, and far away. To lessen the intensity even further, you can make the picture of what you're thinking about grainy and black and white, as though you were viewing it on an ancient television screen. High-definition, colorful movies are more compelling and they inspire people in ways that black-and-white movies cannot.

Remember: make all that is positive in your life big, bright, close, and colorful, and push away all that is negative in your life until it's small, dark, far away, and in black and white.

People often encode their experiences to make the negative ones big and glaringly bright, while their positive experiences are small and much less vivid. Doing so will give those people more negative dispositions because the negative images are so compelling in their minds. Deliberately taking charge of your mind means encoding your experiences and beliefs in the most useful way.

Auditory Qualities of Experiences

Just as the visual qualities of experiences and beliefs affect their intensity, so too do the auditory qualities. Going back to my movie-theater analogy, people have a more intense experience when the sound is loud, engulfing them in stereo surround that is crystal-clear and bass that reverberates within their bodies. Contrast this idea with a movie theater that has low volume and mono sound that's constantly interrupted by popping static. The latter kind of sound is much less compelling than the former, and consequently there is much less feeling associated with it. Listening to a movie in a theater with weak sound is a completely different experience from going to a theater that has powerful sound.

We can deliberately alter our experiences and the power of our beliefs by altering the sound qualities associated with them. By turning the volume up or down and changing the location or pitch of the sound, we can experience feelings differently.

Emotional Qualities of Experiences

By altering the visual and auditory qualities of our beliefs and experiences, we change the feelings associated with them. If you want excellent feelings, you need to see and hear excellent sights and sounds. Now that you understand how to deliberately change your memories, experiences, and beliefs, you can practice making your positive memories even better, your negative memories more neutral, and very powerfully lock in your most empowering beliefs.

How to Change Your Beliefs for Good Using NLP

Now we're going to take what we've learned about beliefs in order to change them—perhaps faster and more effectively than you ever dreamed possible.

Bust the Shy Gene

In earlier chapters, we saw that there really is no such thing as "being" shy or "having a shy gene." So, the first belief that we will change is the belief that you are shy. You are going to take any old thoughts or self-images you may have had about being shy and replace them with thoughts and images of being confident and moving through the world in a whole new way. Don't confine yourself to using this technique for just one belief; you can use it for any beliefs that have been holding you back. Use this method to change whatever beliefs you find less than glorious or less than resourceful.

Read through the instructions a few times to familiarize yourself with what you are about to do. You may also want to get a partner to help guide you through it—someone who is supportive of your transformation, perhaps someone who is on a similar transformational journey. Your partner can read these instructions out to you, or you can simply take note of the instructions and then close your eyes and do it then.

You have certain mental pictures, sounds, and feelings that are associated with beliefs. What we're going to do is change the structure of the belief and thereby change the belief itself. By altering the structure of the belief, we alter how your mind encodes it. The mind encodes powerfully held beliefs differently from weakly held beliefs.

First we will find out how you doubt something—the way in which you encode doubting beliefs in your mind. Then we'll bring you back to your normal, neutral state of being. Third, we'll discover the way in which strong beliefs are encoded in your mind. We'll again bring you back to your normal, neutral state of being. Finally, we will bring about a change in your beliefs. We will take your limiting belief and turn it into a doubt. By doubting your limiting belief, you will free yourself from it. We will then take a new and more empowering belief and lock it into your mind to be held strongly.

Step One: Discover How You Doubt. The first thing to do is close your eyes and think of something that you used to believe in that you no longer do. For example, you might think about how as a child you believed in Santa Claus, which hopefully you no longer do. As you recall that belief, become aware of everything you see that is associated with the belief. More importantly, since we are paying attention to the structure of the belief, look at the different visual qualities of the belief and make note of them.

Regarding what you see and your belief that is no longer true but used to be, answer these questions:

- Is it flat or three-dimensional?
- What size is it?
- Is it clear or out of focus?
- How bright is it?

With your eyes still closed, tune into the sounds that are associated with this belief of yours that is no longer true. Listen closely and pay particular attention to the sound qualities as you answer the following questions:

- Do you hear a voice of doubt?
- Do you hear a voice of authority?
- Do you hear other sounds?
- How loud are the sounds you hear?

Step Two: Break State. Open your eyes, take a deep breath, and name three different things in the room. This will help you shift from a state of doubt back to your neutral state. You might even want to physically move around a little if it helps you return to your neutral, normal state.

Step Three: Discover How You Believe. Think of something that is absolutely true. Pick out something that you have no question about and believe 100 percent to be true. Choose something simple, like "The sun will rise tomorrow" or "I need to breathe air to live." We're going to elicit the same visual and auditory qualities in this powerful belief that we just elicited for the doubting belief.

Just as you did before, when you think about this absolutely true belief, become aware of everything you mentally associate with it. Remember, since we are paying attention to the structure of the belief, look at the different visual qualities of the belief and make note of them.

Regarding what you see and your strongly held belief, answer these questions:

- Is it flat or three-dimensional?
- What size is it?
- Is it clear or out of focus?
- How bright is it?

With your eyes still closed, tune into the sounds that are associated with this belief that is absolutely certain. Listen closely and pay particular attention to the sound qualities as you answer the following questions:

- Do you hear a voice of doubt?
- Do you hear a voice of authority?
- Do you hear other sounds?
- How loud are the sounds you hear?

Step Four: Break State. When you're done making note of all the qualities of what you see and hear, open your eyes, take a deep breath, and name three different things in the room. This will help you shift back to your neutral state. You may want to physically move around a little if it helps you return to your neutral, normal state.

Step Five: Change the Belief. Think of a limiting belief of yours. Since this is a book about confidence, think of one that relates to your confidence or shyness. A good example is: "I can't go up and meet strangers easily." This is a belief that limits many people whose social and business lives would improve if they rid themselves of it.

Once you've selected your limiting belief regarding confidence or shyness, close your eyes and notice all the visual and auditory qualities of that belief. This is just what you've done in Steps One and Three.

After you've gotten the visual and auditory qualities of that belief, begin to change each and every visual and auditory quality of your limiting belief to match all of the visual and auditory qualities of something that you used to believe but no longer do—an old belief. This process recodes your limiting belief, transforming it into something you no longer believe. Make sure that the visual and auditory qualities of the limiting belief match those of the old belief as precisely as possible.

When you're done transforming that belief, open your eyes. Take a deep breath and reorient yourself back into your neutral, normal state of being.

Congratulations on removing a limiting belief! Since nature abhors a vacuum, we will place an empowering belief in your mind where this limiting belief used to reside. To do this, think about something with respect to your confidence that, when you believe it, will improve your life.

Now, as you close your eyes, think of what you want to fully believe in. As you become aware of the visual and auditory qualities of that belief, begin to change its each and every quality to match precisely the visual and auditory qualities of one of your strongest, absolutely true beliefs.

When this process is complete, you will think of this new, empowering belief in the same way that you thought of your other absolutely true, strongly held belief in Step Three. Ensure that the visual and auditory qualities of this new, absolutely true belief and your previous true beliefs match up as much as possible.

Belief Change Pattern

1. Close your eyes.
2. Think about something that you used to believe was true but no longer do.
3. Notice all the visual qualities of that belief.
4. Notice all the auditory qualities of that belief.
5. Notice all the emotional qualities of that belief.
6. Open your eyes and name three different things in the room to clear your mind.
7. Close your eyes.
8. Think about a limiting belief you have, such as "I'm shy" or "I'm not yet confident."
9. Notice all the visual qualities of that belief.
10. Notice all the auditory qualities of that belief.
11. Notice all the emotional qualities of that belief.
12. Open your eyes and name three different things in the room to clear your mind.
13. Adjust your limiting belief to resemble something you used to consider true but no longer do.

I encourage you to practice changing your beliefs and experiences. You'll be surprised at how easy and effective it is!

Use Expectancy to Your Advantage

What you expect tends to be realized more often than you might think. Resourceful people have different beliefs from those who are not resourceful. Resourceful people expect to be able to find a way to achieve their outcome. They expect to be able to easily and naturally form a rapport with anyone they meet. When they want something to happen, they often go for it; and if they make a mistake, they learn from the feedback. These expectations tend to influence a resourceful person's outcome.

Believing the following ideas will increase your interpersonal skills and personal effectiveness. When you meet people and you want to create rapport, remember these beliefs:

- People automatically like you because you are a good person.
- You can easily and naturally meet anyone you choose.
- You can have instant rapport with anyone you choose using these techniques.
- You have a lot in common with any person you meet.
- You can learn something from each and every person you speak with.

You may be thinking that these beliefs are not necessarily true, and if so, you would be correct. However, *we're out to get a result, not to logically prove what is and isn't true.* The above beliefs are useful generalizations that will help you when you believe them.

In all interpersonal relations, assume that you can get and maintain a rapport. Operate under the belief that you have far more in common with the person than not, and you will easily connect with him or her.

Defuse Limiting Beliefs with the Power of Questions

The following method uses questions that are designed to break up limiting beliefs. These questions help you reconnect with your confidence resources. Remember that you have confidence within you at all times. You have successfully been confident in the past. The key is to summon the necessary confidence whenever you choose.

If you're hesitating or behaving tentatively, ask yourself, "What's stopping me from doing what I want?" Once you have the answer to this question, you can transform your frame of mind, your internal dialogue, and your physiology into a state of confidence.

If in fact you do find yourself acting shy, never beat yourself up over it. Remember that there is a positive intention behind every behavior. That means that the way you were acting served a purpose that ultimately did some good in the past. Figure out what the positive intention of your shy behavior is by asking yourself, "What is the positive intention of this tentative feeling?" Be silent and allow the genuine answer to pop into your mind.

When you get an answer, take note of it and then remind yourself that shyness is an outdated way of behaving and that you will choose confidence from here onward. Be good to yourself at all times. Never ask yourself a question like, "Why am I shy?" Asking questions like that will only keep you stuck, because your unconscious mind will come back to you with answers about why you are shy, thus reinforcing the shyness even further. That's the last thing you want.

You want to ask questions that reconnect you to your resources of confidence. Ask yourself, "What would it be like if I were feeling unstoppably confident right now?" How would you feel different? How would you look out at the world as a supremely confident person? By merely answering those empowering questions, you will be forced to access a state of confidence, thereby meeting your desired outcome.

7

Unstoppable Confidence in Personal Relationships

Do unto others as they would like to have done unto them.
—The Platinum Rule

INTERPERSONAL SKILLS ARE FUNDAMENTAL TO gaining unstoppable confidence. Simply knowing these interpersonal skills will dramatically increase your confidence. Because you know how people function, you will naturally be able to relate to anyone and everyone easily by the time you finish this book.

Three Universal Characteristics of Friendship

Stop for just a moment and think about your best friend. You can probably picture that person clearly in your mind.

As you hold on to that image, I want you to notice what it is specifically that you like about this person. Chances are, the qualities that you like about your best friend are related to the following three universal characteristics that make people like one another. All friendships are based on:

- Similarity
- Cooperation
- Praise

Similarity

People like people whom they perceive as being similar to themselves. You and your best friend have things in common. These things may include attitudes, beliefs, hobbies, goals, and dreams. More likely than not, you like to do the same things. Furthermore, you and your best friend probably have similar dislikes as well.

The similarity principle can be used to enhance our interpersonal relations and increase our own personal confidence. There is a distinction between true similarity and perceived similarity. True similarity is actually having something in common with someone, while perceived similarity is matching someone's behaviors (e.g., mirroring) so that his or her subconscious mind perceives you as similar. Both kinds of similarity can help you improve your interpersonal relations. (See Part 4 for an exercise using perceived similarity.)

Cooperation

The next ingredient that ensures people will like each other is cooperation. It is an absolute necessity. Without cooperation, there can be no basis for friendship. People who cooperate with you, participate in activities with you, and generally agree with you are undoubtedly more likable to you than people who do not. If someone you consider your friend decides to stop returning your phone calls, starts canceling appointments on you, or is generally uncooperative, it would obviously be difficult to maintain the friendship, no matter how similar you are to the person.

Praise

Praise is the third factor in making one person like another. The importance of praise is obvious. People like to be praised, complimented, and recognized for their achievements. At work, employees often become disgruntled not because they are not compensated well monetarily, but instead because their hard work goes unrecognized. Just as praise unites people in harmony, put-downs and insults divide people. It is much harder to like someone who puts you down than someone who consistently praises you. If your best friend did nothing but insult you, it would quickly dissolve that friendship.

Perceiving Others

How you perceive people will influence how they perceive you. If you love people and enjoy their company, that belief will impact your life tremendously. On the flip side, if you dislike people and generally disdain their company, that belief will affect you in just the same way. The better you can get along with people, the higher quality the life you will lead.

Intention

Let's discuss the concept of intention. Intention is the subtext of the interaction between people. If you intend to connect with someone before beginning to talk with him or her, you will project that intent and that person will unconsciously pick up on it, responding to you more positively than he or she might have otherwise.

People want acceptance. They want to relax and be themselves, free of any judgment. When you set someone else's comfort as one of your outcomes, that person will find himself or herself automatically more comfortable in your presence. The person may not know why he or she feels relaxed around you, but he or she will feel it.

A Positive Frame of Mind

Do the following as an experiment to reveal the influence of your frame of mind. For a week, make yourself believe that all people are unfriendly and don't like to meet new people. Imagine that they don't want to be bothered at all. After temporarily adopting this frame of mind, go out each day or night that week and try to strike up conversations with strangers. It will be difficult because of your frame of mind. What the thinker thinks, the prover proves. Having those preconceived negative beliefs becomes a self-fulfilling prophecy. Once the week is over, purge yourself of that toxic frame of mind.

The following week, adopt the belief that people are perfectly friendly and they love meeting new, dynamic people such as yourself. Furthermore, recognize that you like to get to know new people, since you can learn something new from each and every person you meet. You accept people for who they are, allow them to be themselves, and are free from judging them. After permanently adopting this frame of mind, go out each day or night for the week and notice how easily and naturally you converse with strangers.

One of the many benefits of having confidence is how other people are put at ease when interacting with the confident you. If someone is uptight and ill at ease, other people can sense it, and they may act correspondingly uptight. However, when someone is genuinely comfortable in being himself or herself, others sense it and consequently let their guard down.

While you do these experiments and see for yourself how influential a positive frame of mind is, remember to have fun! Just go and experiment, play, and practice your new skills. Adjust your behavior continually based on the feedback you receive, and eventually you'll find yourself just where you want to be when meeting new people.

Pitfalls to Avoid

There are several pitfalls to avoid as you develop unstoppably confident interpersonal relationships.

Overcome Intimidation

One thing that you may encounter on your journey to connect and click with other people is the feeling of intimidation. Many things can cause a person to feel intimidated, including the beauty, fame, fortune, and social status of others. People possessing these qualities can seem intimidating. It is important to remember, though, that feeling intimidated—like shyness, fear, anxiety, and every other emotion—is the result of a mental process.

Remember who's in control. You are.

If you ever find yourself feeling intimidated while dealing with someone, recognize the feeling as soon as you feel it. By becoming aware of it and identifying it, you can do something about it.

Take a few steps back and look at the big picture. You are two people talking or interacting in some fashion. It's really not such a big deal. The other person is simply a person in the same way that you are simply a person. When you strip away everything else, whoever it is that intimidates you puts their pants on the same way you and I do. Remembering this will eliminate intimidation and help build the unstoppable confidence within you.

In terms of dating, some people always think that the object of their affection is way out of their league. That is utter and complete nonsense. People are people. No one is below or above anyone else. Beautiful people who might intimidate others are simply human beings with beliefs, desires, values, hopes, dreams, fears, and goals like anyone else.

When you think about it that way, doesn't it make it that much easier to interact with people? As you apply these ideas in your life, I think you'll find that it does. If I ever feel intimidated by someone, it's because I'm focusing on the wrong attribute. All of us have extraordinary gifts; if others focused solely on our gifts, they might become overwhelmed and thus intimidated. We're all human beings and we have much, much more in common than we have differences.

If I feel intimidated, it's because I'm not only dwelling on someone's extraordinary gift, but I'm also blowing that person *way* out of proportion. I'm totally exaggerating and making the person seem larger than life. A useful belief in dealing with someone who has the potential to intimidate you is to realize that you have at least *something* in common with every person you meet. People have much more in common with others than they realize. Most people want to be happy, prosperous, take care of their families, enjoy their lives, and have the freedom to pursue what they want.

When you keep these beliefs in your mind as you talk to a person, you will discover the connection between the two of you deepening as a result of your projecting that similarity to the other person.

Beware of Mind Reading

The second pitfall is mind reading. Mind reading occurs when you pretend to understand someone's internal state without actually communicating with that person. People mind-read often, and it is almost always to their detriment.

Sometimes, people will mind-read about what others think of them. I know I've done this from time to time. You may have, too. What someone thinks in his or her mind could be completely different from what you might be mind-reading off the person. If a friend fails to call you back or a customer does not get back to you immediately, he or she might not be interested in you or your project *or* he or she might have just accidentally forgotten. There are many different potential causes for everything, and the only way to verifiably know is to ask someone.

For the next week, practice becoming aware of whether you are mind reading. If you automatically presume to know someone else's private thoughts, stop and ask yourself, "How do I know? Have I asked this person or has this person communicated this to me? Are there other possibilities for why the person is doing a certain behavior?" When you are aware that you are mind reading, stop at once.

Fortunately, we can mind-read in a positive way too. I know that I just told you that mind reading is something less than useful and does not lead to good communication, with everyone running around pretending to read one another's thoughts. However, when you mind-read positively, it can be very useful.

When I was overcoming my shyness, I had difficulty meeting strangers and, in particular, women. I used to mind-read and say, "She won't like me. She wants to be left alone." This led me to be shy, fear rejection, and become incapacitated by my shyness. And then I decided I'd had enough of mind reading negatively. From this point on, I would avoid mind reading or if I was going to mind-read, I would do it positively.

I figure if you are going to mind-read, you may as well do it positively. And when I began doing this, my confidence immediately swelled up. I would mind-read people whom I wanted to meet, telling myself these were their thoughts: "I hope he [as in me] comes over and talks to me. I sure would like to meet a nice, friendly, easygoing guy right about now. How nice would it be for him to come over?" When I thought like this, it more often than not helped me to approach people and meet them. If you're going to use mind reading at all, use it to your benefit!

Respond Resourcefully to Criticism

Now that we've learned to stop assuming people are speaking ill of us, we will learn how to respond resourcefully to criticisms that others have *actually* made to or about us; this is a very useful tool in improving our interpersonal relationships. If someone is stepping off the beaten path and pursuing his or her passions, there will be criticism. It doesn't matter whether the person criticizing you deliberately wants to hold you back or not—the effect of the criticism can be the same either way, if you do not respond to it resourcefully.

Usually criticism of someone going after his or her dreams signifies an element of jealousy or ignorance on the part of the critic. Otherwise, the critical person would be supportive and cheer you on. Recognize before you go after your dreams that you're putting yourself out there to potentially be criticized. Avoid letting that stop you; instead, just understand that it might happen whether it is warranted or not.

Two resourceful responses to criticism are first, ignoring it altogether; and second, mining the criticism for valuable feedback. Make a distinction between the kinds of criticism you receive to determine which response you should utilize. The worst kind of criticism will be from people who are trying to tear you down in order to feel better about themselves. The other kind of criticism comes from people who mean well and do, in fact, have good intentions in wanting you to improve. Remember that people treat you how you've taught them to treat you. For people giving you destructive criticism, inform them that they need to correct their behavior.

In order to respond resourcefully to criticism, there must be some distance between you and the criticism so that you have time to digest it. As you listen to criticism, imagine that you are surrounded by a thick glass barrier that absorbs any negativity or negative emotions from the criticism so that only the useful, positive content of the message seeps through. Other people may see and hear things differently from you and therefore have good suggestions for you on how to improve, which is why you need to be able to receive positive, constructive criticism.

Teach people how to give you good feedback. Good feedback comes in the form of a "sandwich." The structure is: praise for something done well, suggestions for improvement, and more praise for other things done well. When people use the feedback sandwich, the person receiving the feedback feels good while still getting useful ideas on how to improve.

When giving constructive criticism, remember that the more specific the suggestion for improvement is, the more useful the suggestions will be. The constructive criticism should center on how you can improve next time, instead of dwelling on what you did not do so well this time around. Give others feedback in this way and expect the same from them. You'll be far more effective than you imagined.

Show Confidence in Interactions

The following ideas will get you started in demonstrating unstoppable confidence in your interactions with others. More techniques for creating better personal relationships are found in Part 4.

The Platinum Rule

In dealing with people, many have heard of the Golden Rule—but how about the Platinum Rule?

> **The Golden Rule:** Do unto others as you would have them do unto you.
> **The Platinum Rule:** Do unto others as they would like to have done unto them.

When you think about it, the Platinum Rule obviously makes more sense. If someone feels down and you recognize it, you can proactively make that person feel wonderful.

The Magic of Touch

People who are well liked and confident put others at ease in their presence. One method they use to put others at ease and convey a warm feeling is the power of touch. People crave connection with other people. Touching and being touched by others, if applied correctly, can be one powerful way to make a connection. Whether it's a handshake, a congratulatory pat on the back, or a warm hug, people often respond to touch.

An example that demonstrates the power of touch is a study that was conducted with waitresses. The researchers set out to determine how touch would influence the tips the waitresses earned. The first group of waitresses touched each customer while he or she was ordering items off the menu. The second group acted just as friendly, only they didn't touch the customers at all. The researchers found that the waitresses who touched their customers earned tips that were 50 percent higher than those of the waitresses who did not. What this shows is that the customers perceived the waitresses who touched them as more likable and open.

Finally, though, a word of warning: You should apply touch judiciously and appropriately, never in a way that could be misconstrued as sexual or inappropriate. As with all things, use your common sense!

8

Overcoming Obstacles in the Path to Success

In every adversity, there is a seed of equal or greater benefit.
—Napoleon Hill

ALL THE HAPPIEST, MOST FULFILLED, most successful people realize that success is a process. It's the journey of who we become, not simply the end result, that makes it all worthwhile. The achievement of the goal is sweet. But, as with any goal worth achieving, there will likely be setbacks along the way. Viewing those setbacks in the right light can make the difference in your ultimate success.

No Such Thing as Failure

Thomas Edison did more than ten thousand experiments before he perfected the incandescent light bulb. Colonel

Sanders, the founder of the chicken franchise KFC, got 1,009 rejections before someone bought his chicken recipe. When Sylvester Stallone of *Rambo* fame showed up in Hollywood, he went through more than a hundred auditions before someone cast him in a small role.

What all of these people had in common was that they realized there is no such thing as failure; there are only results. After you've been knocked down, the only thing that matters is that you get back up. As Thomas Edison was developing the light bulb, a newspaper reporter came to interview him about his experiments that had "failed." The newspaper reporter inquired as to when the inventor would give up after failing so many times, to which Edison retorted, "Never." The pressing newspaper reporter insisted, "But you keep failing over and over." Edison swiftly responded, "No, what you don't understand is that I haven't failed. I've just found over ten thousand ways *not to* invent the light bulb." This is very true, since he learned from each previous experiment and made corrections based on his findings.

Masters become masters because they make more mistakes. The more mistakes you make, the more distinctions (small pieces of information you learn by doing) you'll get. The more distinctions you have, the more easily you will reach your outcome. Think about that as it applies to your confidence and going after your dreams. Masters are excellent at the fundamentals. They go back and ensure they have gotten the basics down.

If at first you're not successful, be thankful. Some of the least successful people out there had early successes and decided that there was no room for improvement; therefore they became complacent and stagnated.

Compare this to people who fail royally the first few times. These late bloomers have to develop skills to adjust their behavior based on feedback. They tend to develop habits that lead them toward continual improvement. As they develop these habits and begin to succeed, they eventually surpass the early bloomers in productivity.

The Four Major Causes of Blunted Progress

People stop short of achieving success for many different reasons. Being aware of what stops other people can help you to prevent yourself from sputtering out and lets you continue on the road toward living your dreams. A lot of the "reasons" that prevent people from living their dreams are actually excuses. What I challenge you to do is to systematically go through your life and kick out all the excuse "crutches" that you may have been leaning on.

Blow out the crutches permanently so that there can be no choice but success. This is one of the rare times when reducing your options will ultimately gain you more options in the future. Excuses are false options that will only hinder your progress, and since progress is vital to success, you mustn't let anything stand in your way.

The four major causes of blunted progress are:

1. Fear of change
2. Fear of the unknown
3. Fear of success
4. Fear of failure

Fear of Change

People are creatures of habit. A lot of us do the same things over and over again as if every day were a rerun. This can be good in some contexts. Habits simplify our lives; we don't have to consciously think about how to drive a car, open a door, or use a computer every time we do so. On the flip side, habits can become detrimental to our well-being. If we act too much out of habit, we can become automatons and forget to make conscious choices about what we really want to do. Becoming confident is a breach of habit that people may fear, since it involves an entirely new set of behaviors, attitudes, and values that differ from being shy.

It is useful to believe that change is fun and easy. A change for the better leads to personal growth, and personal growth lets you know that you're really alive. It shows that you are not stagnating.

Sometimes at the start of a big change, it may be painful or seem to have negative effects. Always look on the bright side. Think long-term. Dwell on how the difficulty you experience in making the change can only help you down the line. Pretty soon, you'll discover yourself doing these same difficult things automatically. The more you practice, the easier it gets.

Fear of the Unknown

Fear of the unknown is quite common, even though it makes little sense to me. Life inherently has many unknowns. You never know just what might happen. If you did know what to expect all the time, your life would be completely drained of spontaneity and you would never have any enjoyment that wasn't mapped out beforehand. Is it worth wasting your valuable time and energy contemplating the unknown when you can just take it as it comes, with an optimistic attitude?

Of course, it's only natural to make provisions that ensure the worst-case scenario in each situation does not happen— although, if the worst-case scenario should happen, you can always minimize the damages afterward. This is a fundamental shifting in your mind-set here. It's the difference between taking action to prevent or minimize the worst-case scenario and not taking action because you're worried that something bad might happen. It's important to avoid spending time worrying and fearing the unknown. Instead, take action and increase your peace of mind.

Think of life as an adventure or a game where you make up your own rules to play by. If you moved through life with a frame of mind like that, how much more exciting and fun would your life be?

Fear of Success

Some people subconsciously fear success. Their fear paralyzes them, preventing them from taking any positive action. Successful people find ways to overcome this fear, and that's one of the reasons why they are successful.

There is a myth that if you become successful, you have to move to a different neighborhood and lose all of your friends, and the world as you know it will end. If you subscribe to this theory, you are deluding yourself. Success comes in many forms (marital, spiritual, physical, mental, financial, and so on), and it is wonderful. Success is continually rewarding, and all people should know what it's like to be successful in their own right.

Sometimes people shun success because they think it will impose a higher standard on them and consequently put more pressure on them to perform consistently at a higher level. It's true that a higher standard is set. But who says you can't meet expectations once you've raised the bar? You should always expect excellence out of yourself. You deserve to perform at a high level, no matter what the context. If you merely continue to perform adequately, then you are just trying not to lose; but if you continue to perform with excellence, then you are in it to win! Avoid playing the "try-ing not to lose" game; always opt for the "play to win" game instead.

Fear of Failure

Fear of failure stops many people from going after what they want. Some people tend to dwell on what might happen if they fail. They focus their thoughts on what will happen if nothing goes right. When they do that, they picture all sorts of negative hypothetical situations and eventually talk themselves out of doing something that could have been wonderful.

When people venture outside their comfort zones, they need to focus on the potential benefits and remember why it's important to go after them. After all, there is no such thing as failure; there are only results. Some results are better than others. If you get results that you don't like, you'll naturally adjust your behavior based on the results to persist until you achieve your outcome.

To get past the fear of failure, answer the following questions:

- If you knew you couldn't fail at something, what would you do?
- What would you achieve?
- How would your life be different than it is now?

First you must conceive it, then you must believe it, and finally you will achieve it. Your initial answers to these questions are the outcomes you should pursue. Go for it and make them a reality.

Remember that mistakes are a great way to learn. We all make mistakes sometimes. The more we make them, the better off we are, since that means we'll be learning faster than if we weren't making any mistakes at all. As long as you avoid making catastrophic mistakes, the little ones you make can be your best teachers for how to do something the right way. Even if you did nothing and tried your hardest not to make a mistake, mistakes would be impossible to avoid—since doing nothing in and of itself would be a mistake. You are bound to make mistakes once in a while, so let's make the most of them.

One motto I go by is: "Fail forward fast." Keep on making the mistakes and learn from them. Adjust and move on. Then repeat the cycle. Without making mistakes, there is no personal growth. Without personal growth, there is stagnation.

Be Confident About Mistakes

Be confident about your mistakes; they are simply ways in which we learn. This is the success and confidence secret of go-getters all around the world. After each success that they experience, they integrate that success into their identity as further evidence that they are unstoppable. And after each mistake, they think of it simply as a byproduct of their behavior and a learning opportunity. The mistake doesn't cast any doubt on who they are as people.

Many people have their strategies flip-flopped. Instead of integrating their successes as a part of who they are, they dismiss them. That is all wrong! Dismiss the mistakes as flukes, but not your successes.

People downplay their successes with such phrases as "Oh, I just got lucky," or "It was bound to happen sometime." Those phrases absolve the person from any responsibility for taking action and generating the success. Notice these phrases popping up in other people's language and yours too. Then avoid using them ever again. It wasn't luck. It was you!

To get your victories to occur more often, just as soon as you have a major success, visualize yourself having the same results again in many different contexts. When you've got that winning feeling, it's much easier to imagine yourself having the same feeling over and over again in the future. Visualizing the victories in different contexts will help you create the belief that success is part of who you are, not just an isolated incident that occurs from time to time.

Here's how successful people view their mistakes:

- A mistake is simply a function of what you did, not a part of who you are.
- A mistake is something to learn from.
- A mistake lets you know that you should adjust your behavior.

Here's how successful people view their successes:

- Success is a part of who you are. It happened because you are a successful person.
- Success is something to congratulate yourself on and celebrate.
- Success can be built on to reach even greater heights in the future.

The confidence you are rapidly developing can take the form of a snowball. At first, you pack the smallest bit of snow in your hands and make it as dense as possible so that it sticks together. Then you place the small snowball at the top of a great big hill. As you roll the snowball down the hill, the snowball gathers more and more snow and gains momentum. Pretty soon the snowball is unstoppable and it keeps getting bigger, acquiring more snow at a faster rate. That's how your confidence is growing now. You're packing your small snowball and the techniques in this book are pushing that snowball down the hill. With this snowball racing down the hill, you are stepping further and further outside your original comfort zone. You'll be amazed, surprised, and delighted to find how much you enjoy this wonderful personal growth.

Once you adopt the belief that mistakes are your gateway to learning and a natural part of the process, your confidence will immediately begin snowballing faster. What makes the difference between successful, confident people and those who are tentative and do not pursue their dreams is the way that they view their mistakes.

If you want to do something well, it's worth doing poorly at first. That is why taking action is almost always better than not taking action. In taking action, you will either get your outcome or at least learn something, so that you can do things better the next time. If you fail to take action out of fear, you will learn nothing and stay stuck in the same place you were.

The confident mind-set allows you to make as many mistakes as you need to as fast as you possibly can. The key here is to correct what you're doing based on the feedback you get regarding each mistake. By constantly correcting, eventually you will get your desired outcome. After you do succeed, you will learn to integrate that success into your identity as a person of unstoppable confidence.

The tentative mind-set holds that mistakes are bad and should be avoided. As you become more confident in yourself, you'll naturally find how ineffective the tentative mind-set is in terms of going after your dreams. Mistakes are really only a measure of one specific instance of your behavior;

they are not personal evaluations of your worth as an individual. Avoid taking mistakes personally. Instead, learn from
them and move on.

Failure from an Unstoppably Confident Perspective

Confident people are confident because they know that they
can achieve anything they want. How do they know this?
Because they have a history of persisting until they succeed.
Until they win. Until they get what they want. They may
experience temporary setbacks from time to time, but they
always learn something from these and do things differently until they finally achieve their goals. So how do they
do this? Well, I'm reminded of a story that you may have
already heard.

A group of frogs on a farm came across a bucket of milk
that the farmer had accidentally left behind. They dared
each other to jump over the bucket, and they did, over and
over, until one frog misjudged his jump and fell into the
milk. He tried to scramble out of the bucket, but the sides
were too slick and he fell back in. He could hear the other
frogs laughing at him outside. Not only was he in danger
of drowning, but the other frogs that he thought were his
friends were laughing about it! He was determined to get
out, so he swam and jumped and flailed about, and the more
he tried, the more they laughed at him. As he kept it up, all
his motions ended up churning the milk until it became butter. When the butter was thick enough, the frog had enough
leverage to jump out and escape.

What does this teach us? If you want something badly
enough, you will achieve it. No matter what happens, no
matter what anyone says, even if those whom you thought

were your friends tell you otherwise, always know that you can. Refrain from asking yourself questions like "Is it possible?" or "Can I do this?" You already know you can do it! Presuppose it as a given.

You can accomplish whatever you set your mind to accomplish. With the inevitability of achieving your goal already firmly established, ask yourself, "What is it going to take to accomplish my goal?" This question assumes that the possibility of success is already a definite in your mind, and now the only thing to determine is how, specifically, you will get there.

9

Act as If

*Quality questions create a quality life. Successful people ask
better questions, and as a result, they get better answers.*

—Anthony Robbins

So now you may be wondering how to get unstoppable
confidence. We've talked about what confidence is and what
it isn't, as well as about aspects of your language and belief
systems that need changing. But how, exactly, do you get
there? Parts 3 and 4 give you techniques and exercises to
help you change your language—and change yourself. To
get you started, here's the first step to set you on your journey to unstoppable confidence.

Acting as If: An NLP Essential

If you act *as if* something is real for long enough, you will
eventually forget that you are only pretending, and however

you are acting will become your habit—this is one of the keys to neurolinguistic programming. People who used to be shy have used this "as if" frame of mind to develop their confidence. The difference between people who are confident and those who are shy are their habits.

Habits can either be good or bad. The secret is to have a wealth of good habits. The more empowering habits you have, the better your life will be. Developing these habits of behaving confidently can be enjoyable too. It's exciting to witness your personal transformation as you gain more confidence in yourself.

The Pretend It and Have It Technique

The mind and body are part of a cybernetic system; this means that the body influences the mind and the mind influences the body. You can pretend to have confidence by reliving confident experiences in your mind, which will get your body to adopt confident physiology.

Or if you choose to adopt confident physiology, your mind will adjust what you are seeing, hearing, and feeling internally to experience confidence. We can use this to our advantage.

Getting confidence is no different from pretending to have confidence; keep doing it for long enough and pretty soon you'll forget that you're pretending. By the time you've done that, confidence will have become a habit. Following that, your confidence gets ingrained into your personality and it becomes part of your identity.

Remember times as a child when you played make-believe. Children have excellent imaginations and are very good at playing—and consequently, learning. Play make-believe now and pretend that you have the confidence before you really do have it.

Questions About Confidence

Imagine what it would be like to be ten times more confident than you are now, and answer the following questions:

- How would you be moving differently?
- How would your body posture be different?
- How would your inner voice be different?
- How would you be speaking to others?
- What is going through your mind?
- How does your body feel?
- Where in your body do you feel that confidence first?
- How could you intensify that confident feeling in your body?

By answering the questions and doing what they invite you to do, you will see your unstoppable confidence soar. When your confidence soars, forget that you're pretending and take action to do whatever you need to get done.

When I was learning how to walk up to strangers and begin talking, I would ask myself these questions one by one. With each question I answered, I adjusted my behavior to pretend as if I already had the confidence I was seeking. And after answering all the questions, I could actually feel unstoppable confidence within me. This propelled me to introduce myself to strangers and begin talking with them.

The reverse of this technique is also true, so be fore-warned about that. If you think about shyness and adopt shy body language, your mind and body will make you feel shy. If you catch yourself doing this, acknowledge it and then begin asking yourself the confidence questions, which are designed to get you into a superconfident state.

Now work your way through the techniques and strategies in Parts 3 and 4. Before long, you won't be *acting* unstop-pably confident, you'll *be* unstoppably confident.

PART 3

The Language of
Unstoppable Confidence

10

Mastering Your Internal Voice

Make a game of finding something positive in every situation.
Ninety-five percent of your emotions are determined by how
you interpret events to yourself.

—Brian Tracy

IMAGINE A PRIVATE RADIO STATION in your mind that broadcasts just for you. If the DJ put on a record that played a whining, droning voice—constantly cataloguing your failures and griping about how hard life is—you'd feel pretty bad, wouldn't you? Wouldn't you want to turn it down—or fire the DJ? Conversely, what if you could listen to a rich, warm voice, reminding you about all the great accomplishments of your life, the things that make you happy and thankful, the goals and dreams that you have? Wouldn't that feel just great? Wouldn't you want to listen to it a lot, with the volume high enough for you to feel it vibrate throughout your body?

That is exactly what we are going to do in this chapter. By mastering some basic NLP techniques, you are going to learn to use your internal voice to positively change your state of mind and direct your thoughts in resourceful ways, no matter how you have been using your voice in the past. You will master your internal voice so that your state of mind becomes and stays absolutely fabulous.

Squashing Negative Internal Dialogue

Many people have a negative internal voice that constantly eats away at them. This negative internal dialogue often dwells on the bad things in life and is quick with a put-down or some other nasty comment. Consequently, it's difficult for people to move ahead if they don't first conquer their negative internal voice.

This kind of inner monologue can cause a negative self-fulfilling prophecy; if you let it rule your mind, it will also rule your world. What occurs far too frequently is that the negative internal dialogue discourages someone from doing something bold and constructive. Then, if this person attempts to take the initiative and fails, the internal voice rubs it in. This further drives home the false belief that the person cannot do whatever he or she sets out to do. The negative internal voice then becomes more powerful because it was "right" before, and it incapacitates the person again the next time he or she dares to step outside of the comfort zone. This cycle must be stopped.

Considering all of this, how would you like to silence this negative internal voice once and for all?

First, identify the qualities of your negative internal monologue by answering the questions listed here. When you're aware of the specific qualities of your negative internal voice, you can more easily silence it.

- Whose voice do you hear?
- Where does the voice seem to come from?
- At what level is the volume of the voice?
- Does the voice speak rapidly or slowly?

Now that you are more consciously aware of the voice than ever before, we can squash it. To do this, you must actively choose to change the qualities of your internal voice. You can do this by imagining the same voice with its vocal properties altered.

Sometimes the negative internal voice is that of one or both of your parents. Sometimes the negative internal voice is your own. What would happen if you took the voice and made it sound like, say, Mickey Mouse's voice? It would be hard to take that high-pitched voice seriously, right?

What would happen if you made it another favorite childhood cartoon character's voice, or perhaps a clown's voice? Don't take my word for it; do it yourself to find out. The next time you recognize a negative internal voice, mentally repeat what it just said in the voice of Bozo the Clown. You might be surprised to discover how quickly an internal voice that used to keep you stuck becomes meaningless when it sounds like this.

What happens if you change where the negative internal voice comes from? Put the voice in different locations and farther away to lessen its impact. Picture a voice coming out of your kneecap, softly taunting you about your shortcomings. Notice how this changes things.

What happens when you speed the voice up so very fast that it's almost incomprehensible, like a record turned up to 180 RPM? What happens when you slow the voice down so much that it's deep and distorted? You can adjust your internal voice as though it has a volume dial, turning the volume up or down to suit the situation. Most likely, the quieter the voice, the less influence it will have. Find what works best for you, and use it to thwart the impact of that pesky, negative internal voice.

The underlying foundation of this technique is the idea that you can consciously direct your mind instead of just allowing it to function on impulse. With the techniques I've outlined, you will be consciously directing how you hear your internal voice. I bet you're feeling better about having more control over your negative internal voice, and that voice is having less and less of an impact on you.

Amplifying Positive Internal Dialogue

As inhibiting as a negative internal voice is, a positive internal voice can be twice as effective in leading you to greatness. Everything that we did in the last section to de-emphasize the negative internal monologue, we'll now learn to do in reverse to amplify the positive internal monologue.

When you hear positive, encouraging words inside your mind, take a moment and silently thank yourself. Eventually you won't feel the need to do so, but when you first feel the confidence of a positive interior voice, congratulations are in order! As your internal voice bursts forth with positive words, reinforce them with the appropriate behaviors. The more you reward yourself for acting in the way you want, the more you will find yourself automatically acting in the way you want. You won't even have to make it a point to do so—it will simply become a reflex.

Your ideal internal dialogue should be in your own voice. The reason for this is that you and you alone run your life and make the decisions. If the internal dialogue has the voice of anyone other than you, you are effectively relinquishing your personal power to that person. Since you are the one running your mind and your life, reclaim them both by making the internal dialogue yours alone forever. Simply replace the current "voice of authority" in your life with your own voice.

Let your own positive voice resonate within. Allow it to spread throughout your whole body. Whenever you hear that glowing, positive internal voice, let it boom from within you like it's coming from the largest speakers you've ever heard at the loudest volume imaginable. The louder the volume, the more vividly the feeling will course throughout your entire being. So when you want to really feel it, crank up the volume!

While your positive internal voice shows up more and more often, sometimes it will give you a positive statement disguised in question form. An example is: "You can do it?" The tone may be questioning, yet deep down this sentence is a statement. Ratchet up the power of your internal voice by turning the sentence into a statement: "You can do it."

Repeat it in your mind a few times, if you need to. Next, make your internal voice even stronger by converting the statement into the exclamation, "You can do it!" Shout this inside your mind so there can be no doubt.

Find Your Passion

Your confidence will grow with each and every technique that you add to your repertoire. The more your confidence grows, the more you will discover how much you want to reconnect with your passions and go after your dreams. In doing this, ask yourself, "If money were no object and you knew you could not fail, what would you do in your life?" The immediate answer to this question is your passion and what you should do with your life.

Using the techniques you're learning in this book, stamp out the negative internal voice that might try in vain to crop up. Find your passion, set your goals, and then take immediate, repeated, massive action that will virtually guarantee your success. Commit to yourself that you will never quit. Remind yourself that you have quit quitting, and move ahead into the life you want and deserve to have, now.

11

Speaking the Languages of Confidence

Dedicate yourself to the good you deserve and desire for yourself. Give yourself peace of mind. You deserve to be happy. You deserve delight.

—Mark Victor Hansen

NOW THAT WE'VE MASTERED OUR internal voices, it's time to turn our attention to our externals—how we project our internal dialogues to the outside world.

The Vocabulary of Confidence

If you listen to other people talking, you will notice that those who are confident use a certain vocabulary—and those lacking in confidence seem to draw their words and phrasing from an entirely different dictionary. Most people don't give a lot of thought to the language they use. As such, people's habitual language patterns reflect back on their thinking, be it confident thinking or a lack thereof.

Not only does language reflect a person's thinking, but it also reinforces a person's thinking. The key is to use the following information for transforming your everyday vocabulary. When this occurs, you'll not only change your thinking, you'll change your life!

So, what are these changes? I have assembled two sets of words that you must take into account when speaking. First, there is a set of words that you absolutely need to eliminate from your vocabulary. Then there's a set of words that you need to memorize and integrate into your speech in order to project maximum confidence. It is hard to overstate the importance of sending the right signals with your language, but it's easier to learn to do so than you may think. Let's get down to it.

The Confidence Killers

First, we'll tackle the set of words that you need to eliminate and completely remove from your vocabulary. If you catch yourself using these words, say, "Hey, wait a minute. I'm no longer shy. There's a better word for that."

Don't beat yourself up if you hear yourself using one of these words. Just acknowledge that you used the word in the past, and increase your efforts to eliminate it from your vocabulary in the future.

Try

The first word is *try*. Have you ever heard someone "try to do" something? There's a difference between trying to do something and actually doing something. Quite simply, trying is lying.

In *Star Wars*, Yoda said, "There is no try, only do." Yoda was right on the money. There *is* no try. If you ask someone to do you a favor and the person says, "I'll try," you can count on him or her not doing the favor for you. Otherwise the person would say, "I'll do it."

The word *try* communicates a "maybe" attitude in a world that craves certainty. Instead, use the word *do*. Say, "I will do it." Eliminate the word *try*. Don't *try* to eliminate the word *try*, do it!

> **The Shy Sentence:** I'll try to do the laundry tomorrow.
> **The Confident Sentence:** I will do the laundry tomorrow.

Hope

Another word that is not for confident people is *hope*. Now, *hope* is a nice and pleasant word. However, it announces a lack of action. For example, "I hope things get better," or "I hope my situation resolves itself." Contrast this with: "I'm going to make it happen" or "I'm going to make my situation better." Hoping for something to happen is being reactive, whereas taking action and expecting success is proactive.

> **The Shy Sentence:** I hope I can take a trip to Hawaii someday.
> **The Confident Sentence:** I am making plans to take a trip to Hawaii next year.

But

But negates every word that precedes it in the sentence. An example is: "I want to go to a movie but I have a lot to do." In this example, it sounds as if the person will not be going to the movie. When someone hears the word *but*, he or she immediately knows that what was just said should be disregarded.

If you want to communicate the same thing without using the word *but*, substitute the phrase *and yet*.

> **The Shy Sentence:** I want to go but I have something else going on.
>
> **The Confident Sentence:** I want to go and yet I have something else going on.

The Three "Oulds": Would, Could, and Should

As Dr. Seuss might have said if he were concerned with confidence, here are three "oulds" that are no good. As we go through each "ould" we'll discover how its usage in some places decreases confidence, and we'll learn how to replace them with words that will propel you even further to success.

Would. *Would* is a conditional word. It's not confident. It's not absolute. When I was discussing the notion of writing a book, some people said, "Yeah, I would write a book too if . . . ," and then they'd give some reason that supposedly precluded them from writing a book. Well, *would* is conditional and presupposes there's something standing in the way of success. It's pointless to use the word *would*, because nothing can stop a confident person from achieving success. Eliminate that word from your vocabulary.

> **The Shy Sentence:** I would talk to that stranger now if only . . .
>
> **The Confident Sentence:** I will talk to that stranger now.

Could. If someone says, "I could go meet that person," then my question is, "What's stopping you?" Using the conditional word *could* implies that there's an uncertainty attached to your action. For example, "I could go meet that person," or "I could go market my business to ten new people and expand it." Just as we've seen with the word *would*, *could* also suggests that there's something preventing you from achieving your goal.

Could implies that there's a chance, but the message it sends is "don't count on it." Eliminate it from your vocabulary. It's much better to use a more definite phrase, such as *I can* or *I can't*.

> **The Shy Sentence:** I could try making a speech in front of my peers.
> **The Confident Sentence:** I can make a speech in front of my peers.

Should. *Should* is the worst of the "oulds." *Should* implies expectations and limited options. Think of the sentence, "I should be doing this right now." Well, you should be doing this according to whom? Ask yourself that. Whose expectations? It's all about your own expectations, your own internal frame of reference. After all, you're running the show; you're leading your own life. You're a unique individual in charge of what you're doing. Saying "should" is like keeping yourself hostage by limiting your choices.

If you have a preconceived notion that you should always do a certain thing in a given circumstance, then you're not going to investigate other options because you're just going to do what you "should." And that's a limiting perspective, because whenever you have fewer choices, you have less control over your life. Confident people don't have that problem, regardless of whether or not the situation dictates they "should."

> **The Shy Sentence:** It's late and I should get home now.
> **The Confident Sentence:** It's late and I choose to go
> home now.

The Confidence Builders

Now that we have talked about the words that we are eliminating from our vocabulary, let's discuss the words that will skyrocket your confidence when you integrate them into your daily thoughts and speech. The underlying principle is definition of purpose: words that show confidence and let people know what you want.

Here are the words and phrases to add to your vocabulary for enhanced confidence:

- Absolutely
- Definitely
- Positively
- Assuredly
- Without a doubt
- Of course
- Certainly
- Undoubtedly
- Obviously
- Guaranteed
- Naturally
- Sure

What do all of these words do? They communicate a message: "There's absolutely no doubt in my mind that this is the way it is." Now, as you begin to use these words, notice how people respond to you, because they will respond differently.

If someone asks, "What do you want to do?" there are a number of responses.

Here are two examples.

> **The Undecided Sentence:** We should do something fun, I hope.
> **The Confident Sentence:** I absolutely want to see a movie tonight.

You will notice the difference between someone who is confident and wants to do something and someone who may want to do something, yet is too shy to say what that might be.

The Language of Motivation

Now let's talk about how to use language to motivate yourself to do what you want. You can take any task or action that you don't particularly care about and crank up your motivation, so that you just have to do it.

Modal Operators

This goes back to our use of language and how it shapes our model of the world. With this technique, we will focus on an aspect of language called *modal operators*. When you listen to someone's language, and especially his or her use of modal operators, you'll hear so much about how that person moves through the world and the source of his or her motivation.

So what are modal operators? They are words like *must, have to, need to, will, can, should, would,* and so on. For our purposes, they fit into three categories: necessity, possibility, and impossibility.

Modal Operators of Necessity. Modal operators of necessity indicate that something is necessary and that something needs to be done. They are words such as:

- Have to
- Need to
- Must
- Mandatory
- Required

As such, using them in the right places in our language is excellent for motivation:

- "I have to take a break."
- "You need to go do some training."
- "We must work on this project now."
- "It's mandatory that you do your confidence exercises regularly."

Modal Operators of Possibility. Modal operators of possibility are words such as:

- Can
- Could
- Might
- Possibly
- Maybe

These words open up possibilities to us. When we use them correctly in our language—as modal operators, not as one of the dreaded "oulds"—they imply choice:

- "We have so many options we can pursue."
- "I could make it at 9:30 P.M. sharp. Easy."
- "Perhaps we might consider the new developments?"

Modal Operators of Impossibility. Then we have modal operators of impossibility. These are words that imply that we simply cannot do something. *Cannot* is just one of those words:

- Cannot
- Will not
- Must not

Notice how modal operators of impossibility close off options that may have been available to us:

- "I'll never go back to that old way of being."
- "You must not neglect to follow these instructions carefully."
- "I can't go a day without doing my unstoppable-confidence exercises!"

How to Easily Motivate Yourself

So how do we use the knowledge of these modal operators to crank up our motivation? We do this by simply chaining them together. I want you to follow along in this example.

We will begin by saying a set of phrases. Each of them will differ in just a few subtle but powerful ways. Now for the purposes of this exercise, for you to fully experience the impact of this technique, I want you to say each of these phrases out loud, confidently and powerfully. Take on a confident physiology; sit up straight and say these phrases with an authoritative tone of voice.

We will begin by thinking for a moment about taking tomorrow off from work (or if it's a weekend as you read this, taking off the upcoming Monday). Notice what it's like, notice how you feel as you think about this now. Your motivation, your beliefs about whether or not you can do this, will be influenced by how you say the words in this exercise to yourself.

Now I want you to say to yourself, "I *can't* take tomorrow off," and notice how you feel about taking the day off tomorrow. (*Can't* is a modal operator of impossibility in the present tense.)

Now say, "I *couldn't* take tomorrow off." Notice how using a modal operator of impossibility closes off that option.

Then say the following sentence: "I *can't* take tomorrow off."

As you fully assume confident physiology, say aloud, "I *couldn't* take tomorrow off." While you do this, notice how that feels to you internally. Each time we exchange one of these modal operators for the other, the feeling will change.

Next, say aloud, "I *could* take tomorrow off." Using the word *could* will alter your experience as you find that saying it produces a different feeling. You might compare and contrast the differences between all of these sentences and think about how one word can so drastically alter the meaning and feeling of the sentence. *Could* shifts your thinking from that of impossibility into thinking that something is possible, albeit with conditions attached. To paraphrase the sentence, you could take tomorrow off if some condition were met. The conditional aspect is implied through the usage of the word *could*, as I explained earlier.

Now say the same sentence, replacing *could* with *can*. "I *can* take the day off tomorrow." Your thinking has been shifted from the possibility of taking tomorrow off, if some condition were met, to a very real possibility in your mind that you, in fact, can take tomorrow off if you choose.

To amplify this possibility, next replace the modal operator in the sentence with *may*. Say to yourself out loud, "I *may* take tomorrow off."

May presupposes that you may or may not take the day off. *May* implies not only the fact that you can do something, but suggests that you are considering whether or not to do it.

We've now gone from absolute impossibility to serious consideration regarding taking the day off!

Now use the next modal operator: "I *should* take the day off tomorrow."

Next, say to yourself out loud, "I *shall* take the day off tomorrow." This exercise has taken you from conditional to probable to almost certain. You're finally making a commitment to yourself to take the day off tomorrow because you deserve it. (After all, don't you?)

Next, tell yourself, "I *have to* take the day off tomorrow." Really say it, like your sanity depends on it, and notice how much more powerful the expression becomes. When you say, "I *have to* take the day off tomorrow!" you can feel it course through every part of you.

Next, say, "I *need to* take the day off tomorrow." You *need to*. Taking a day off has gone from being a requirement to a necessity, a fundamental need. Notice how these tiny differences increase your motivation that much more.

Finally, use the modal operator we've all been waiting for: "I *will* take the day off tomorrow." Say it authoritatively and powerfully. Notice how committed you are to taking the day off tomorrow. Look at how much your motivation has changed, just because you've changed each word on the continuum of motivation. You've come from a place where

it was absolutely impossible to take the day off to being committed to taking the day off tomorrow.

This example demonstrates the power of these words and
how people are using these words to either limit themselves
(modal operators of impossibility), to motivate themselves
(modal operators of necessity), or to empower themselves with
more options (modal operators of possibility).

12

The Body Language of Confidence

If we are to have magical bodies, we must have magical minds.
—Dr. Wayne Dyer

BODY LANGUAGE IS JUST AS important as verbal language. Your internal images, sounds, and emotions affect your physiology—and vice versa.

Confident Body Language vs. Shy Body Language: A Quick Lesson

Confident and shy body language differ greatly and are rarely mistaken for each other. By realizing the difference, you can be sure to maintain confident body language as you build unstoppable confidence.

Here are some examples of shy body language:

- Hanging your head as if ashamed of yourself
- Slumping your shoulders forward
- Drooping your spine instead of standing up straight
- Looking down at the ground

Having confident body language is just as easy to spot, but it sends a much better message. Here are some examples of confident body language:

- Keeping your head held high
- Having your shoulders thrust back
- Keeping your abdominal muscles tucked in
- Standing up tall and proud

Even if you don't feel confident at any given moment, you can project confidence through your words, gestures, and body language.

Avoid Wimpy Gestures

Some people resort to blaming and placating in stressful situations. Rather than communicating their willingness to find a way out of a situation, they become panicked and are only concerned with who's at fault. These people clearly lack confidence. If they were to alter their behavior by maintaining powerfully confident physiology, their internal states would match that of a calm, cool, and collected person.

Maintaining composure is much more resourceful and effective for solving a problem than blaming and placating ever could be. Here are some methods for how to move your body to stay confident.

Never Use Placating Gestures

Confident people never make placating gestures. These gestures convey that you are inferior or submitting to another person. A classic placating gesture is when someone shrugs her shoulders with palms facing upward, as if pleading, "I didn't do it." This conveys a need to absolve oneself of responsibility for a situation. In order to have unstoppable confidence, you must avoid these gestures at all times.

Another placating gesture is the shrug, which means that someone doesn't really know what's happening—or perhaps doesn't even care. It does not make any sense to convey that you don't know or care about a situation. If you don't know about something, simply admit as much in a matter-of-fact way. People who lack confidence often give an exaggerated response, announcing in an annoyed tone that they have no clue.

A lot of times you can find the answer to problems if you stop for a moment and think about potential solutions, instead of giving up so easily and pleading ignorance. Henry Ford said, "Thinking is the hardest activity there is to do. That is why so few people engage in it." People who are confident may not necessarily have the answer, yet they know they have all the resources to find the answer.

When I ask someone a question and the immediate response is "I don't know," it indicates to me that this person is not even willing to make an educated guess or take the initiative to find out the answer. A better response when you genuinely do not know is to say, "I'm not sure yet." This indicates the truth about your uncertainty and presupposes that you will probably be sure sometime in the future, as indicated by the word *yet*.

Never Use Blaming Gestures

The opposite of placating is blaming. Unstoppably confident people never do this. Blaming takes place when you are accusing someone else in your stead. The blaming frame of mind is a very negative frame, and it does not empower you at all. The classic gesture associated with blaming other people is pointing fingers—and as some people learn when they're young, when your pointer finger is aimed at someone else, there are three other fingers pointing right back at you. Too many people blame, and it's not useful.

Confident people come from a place of wanting to find solutions. They look for options on how to solve problems and create solutions. They move through the world calm, cool, and unperturbed by outside events. They manage their emotions rather than letting their emotions manage them.

Avoiding both blaming and placating gestures will help you be who you are: an unstoppably confident person who solves problems and gets the job at hand done efficiently. Who or what caused the situation is irrelevant. The main idea is to solve it and prevent it from occurring again in the future.

Practice Unstoppable Body Language

If you want to feel like you are the most charismatic person around, project good thoughts outward. They will manifest themselves in your body language.

Walk Confidently

Confident people have a certain walk. When they enter a room, it seems as though they belong there—or even as though they own the place! As you practice walking confidently, remember that the situation is whatever you make it. Keep your head held high, your shoulders back, your tummy tucked in, and move through the world with deliberate steps. Feel free to walk at your own pace instead of adopting the speed everyone else is using. Avoid shuffling your feet or looking down at the ground. You'll notice a difference as you practice your confident body language and pay attention to the way you walk.

Steeple Your Hands for Confidence

Steepling is a gesture that conveys confidence. Press your fingertips together while keeping your palms separate, touching each of your fingertips to the fingertip on the opposite hand. Many unstoppably confident people steeple their hands to exude confidence. In fact, so many confident people do it that the gesture is now associated with confidence. Get in the habit of steepling your hands when you want to convey confidence to others.

The Wonder of Smiling

If you want more confidence, all you have to do is smile. Practice smiling with anyone you see, anywhere you go! Do it when you're at work, at home, or in the store. No matter where you are, give someone the gift of a smile. As you make it a habit to smile, practice making small talk with people. You'll soon discover your conversations flow-ing with greater ease than ever before. Ask people how they are doing. Ask about their weekends. Find out what they want in life. People love to talk about themselves, and it feels good to really listen intently to someone else.

Even for me, at the depths of my shyness, smiling was a very effective technique. Being a naturally happy guy, I smiled often at people just because the mood struck me. What I discovered is that when I smiled at people, they would naturally smile back. In fact, I'd even make a game out of it: how many people could I get to smile? Sometimes, when someone didn't respond to my smile as I approached, I'd keep broadening my smile until the person finally broke out of his or her stoic facial expression and smiled back.

Smiling is disarming; it puts other people at ease. Since giving a smile is absolutely free and always feels good to either give or receive, you should smile as often as possible.

The Sound of Confidence

Another key to confident communication is having excellent vocal tonality. Vocal tonality is the pitch at which you speak. If your voice is nasal, for example, it will be irritating. Irritating other people is certainly not good when your goal is to project a confident image while communicating with them. You want tonality that resonates within other people and causes them to feel good. Most people aren't even aware of it, but your vocal tonality has an effect on all people at the unconscious level. Speaking with bad tonality is like running fingernails down a chalkboard. Personally, I'd rather listen to a dental drill than listen to someone drone on with nasal tonality.

Tonality Exercise. The good news is that people can improve their tonality through repeated practice. In this exercise, you will place your hands on a certain body part and place your attention there while speaking. As a result, you will notice a shift in tonality, and by the end of the exercise, you'll have a deep, resonant tonality.

Place your hands on your nose and say, "This is my nose." The tonality should be nasal now and probably very irritating.

Move your hands down to your mouth now and say, "This is my mouth." As you do this, listen for the difference in your tonality already.

Next, place your hands on your throat as you say, "This is my throat." Hear the change in your tonality yet?

Place your hands on your upper chest and declare, "This is my chest." Notice your tonality becoming more resonant?

Finally, place your hands on your abdomen and say, "This is my abdomen. When I talk like this, I get a deep, rich tonality that people enjoy."

Where your attention goes, the energy flows, and that is the reason why your tonality gets better when you concentrate on your abdominal area. If you want to listen to and model your tonality after someone, turn on the radio and really concentrate on how the disc jockeys use their voices. You'll never find a disc jockey with a nasal voice, for reasons mentioned before.

The Look of Confidence

Confident people are able to look others straight in the eye and tell it like it is. By looking someone in the eye, you will be perceived as being more sincere, genuine, and honest—no matter what you are saying—than if you are shifty-eyed or avoiding eye contact. People who lack confidence tend not to look others directly in the eye. This elicits suspicion from the person with whom the nonconfident person is interacting, because most people, when they are telling the truth, look others directly in the eye. If you have nothing to hide, focus your attention on looking people in the eye. You can even practice feeling good while you do it.

If you have a tendency right now to avoid eye contact, that's just fine. Call it a starting point. After you do the following exercise, you will discover how easily and naturally you can do it. By the end of this exercise, you will have formed the beginning of a habit. The difference between confident people and shy people, in summary, is that confident people have habits that cause them to behave confidently. Conversely, shy people have habits that cause them to act shy.

Eye Contact Exercise. This exercise is designed to give you the ability to "be present" with someone and look that person straight in the eye, giving you more confidence. You'll need a partner for this exercise; a great partner would be a supportive friend, spouse, or relative. Read through all of the directions first and then begin. By doing this exercise you'll naturally find yourself breaking through limits as your confidence rises to unprecedented levels.

Set an outcome for what you want to get out of this exercise. One good outcome is to be able to look people in the eye anytime, tell them anything you choose, and feel at ease while you're doing it.

Get a timer that will let you know when five minutes is up. What you are going to do is sit across from your partner in complete silence and "be present" with him or her. All you have to do is be silent and look the person straight in the eye.

Beware! This is harder than it sounds. As you do this exercise, you may have certain urges to laugh or look away. That only means that you now have an opportunity to break through previously held limits. Stay with the exercise and continue to look your partner in the eye. Meanwhile, your partner will be doing the same with you. If you do laugh or glance away, your partner should gently say, "Stop. Be present. Start again." Similarly, if your partner laughs or glances away, give him or her the same instruction. Continue on like this for the entire five minutes.

Having this skill means that you can confront any person and be there for him or her as a good listener. Your direct eye contact with another person means you're neither superior nor inferior. You are merely two equals communicating on level ground.

Do this exercise with your partner as many times as you feel you need to in order to be able to look at someone. Pretty soon, what you'll discover is that it is really very easy to do so. You will no longer be intimidated by direct eye contact.

The real world is the true test to gauge how far you've come. After doing the exercise, practice it in the real world and notice how easily you do it. How surprised will you be when you find yourself doing it automatically? Others will react positively to your new confidence. This eye contact that you've learned is not designed to intimidate, but to foster better communication through honesty and openness. It will also let other people know that you have the look of confidence.

PART 4

Becoming Unstoppable

13

Twenty-One Explosive Techniques to Supercharge Your Confidence

First comes thought, then organization of that thought into ideas and plans, then transformation of those plans into reality. The beginning, as you will observe, is in your imagination.

—Napoleon Hill

THE TECHNIQUES, EXERCISES, AND STRATEGIES in this chapter will speed you on your way to unstoppable confidence. Practice them regularly and watch your confidence soar!

TECHNIQUE 1: The Instant Shift

One of the major steps in gaining more confidence is being aware of when you're lacking confidence. The reason for this is that you have to be aware of something before you can change it. When you're aware that you're not being confident, you can change it. It will no longer be a given that you're shy or tentative or whatever label you previously used to describe yourself. As you become conscious of what your mental process is with respect to confidence, pay particular attention to your internal voice. If you have a limiting, negative voice nagging at you, I'm sure you naturally realize how that can stop you dead in your tracks when you really want to go for it.

While you're paying attention to your internal voice, notice what sorts of images are inside your mind. What you hear and see internally impacts how you feel, and the way you feel either frees you to take action or holds you back. When I was locked in my dungeon of shyness, any time I wanted to go out and meet a woman, I would project a big picture of women rejecting me and laughing at me before I even said hello. With these images in my mind, I was completely paralyzed with fear and took no action. Instead, I watched opportunity pass me by, and I regretted it every time.

If you want excellent feelings, you have to see and hear excellent things, which is easy because you are in control of your own mental processes. Whenever you're acting shy, you must simply stop and realize that it's a process—and that you can change it. If you find yourself acting in a tentative or shy way, here are some NLP techniques you can try.

• **Interrupt the Process.** Imagine a police officer springing up inside your mind, holding a red stop sign. Imagine that he shouts out in an authoritative tone as loud as he can, "STOP!" When you hold this image in your mind, you'll find yourself immediately stopping the process of feeling that you lack confidence.

• **Shift Your State.** Once you stop the process, you can change directions and go in any direction you want. For our purposes, you should immediately shift your physical state to one that exudes confidence. Employ excellent physiology and posture: head up, shoulders back, stomach tucked in. Put that smile on your face and feel good. Just like that. If your body is in a state of confidence, it's easy for you to mentally follow suit.

The Instant Shift

1. Recognize your shy or unconfident action.
2. Interrupt the process.
3. Shift your physical state to a confident posture.
4. Let your mind follow suit.

TECHNIQUE 2: Rehearse Confidence

Once you interrupt a negative mental process, you can then consciously choose the emotional state you want to experience. You won't be merely acting out of habit; you'll be acting out of a conscious choice, and that is very powerful. With this technique, you can program yourself to have unstoppable confidence whenever you need it.

The key is that what you rehearse is what you get. A friend of mine who is into martial arts always reminds me to "train the way you fight because you will fight the way you train." This holds true for being confident as well. By rehearsing confidence in your mind, you will have it when you need it.

For you to have unstoppable confidence, you need to mentally rehearse it in the present. This means we are going to visualize what we desire—confidence. We will watch ourselves walking, talking, and moving confidently. We will see ourselves doing things that before we did not even realize were possible.

If it's difficult to do this at first, don't worry. Visualizing is a skill like any other, and you will get better at it with practice. If you think you have difficulty visualizing, pretend that it's easy for you. One way to deal with anything is to fake it until you make it. Pretend that you can visualize and as you do that, you will develop such skill in visualizing that pretty soon you'll forget that you're just pretending and you will be a great visualizer.

Now that you're visualizing, focus in on the image of yourself behaving confidently, as projected on your mental movie screen. Notice how you exude confidence from every fiber of your being and how others can sense it coming from you. As you see yourself behaving confidently, listen to what you hear as you fully experience that ultimate state of confidence within. To amplify your confident state, make the picture bigger, brighter, and closer. Crank the sound way up in your mind so that you can feel the confidence coursing throughout your entire being. Let the bass resonate all throughout your body. When you make these adjustments to your experience, notice how much more powerful and confident you become.

Do this exercise as many times as it takes to thoroughly feel the confidence inside you. How will you know when you've done it enough? The answer is that by looking at the mental image of your confident self, you'll automatically feel the confidence. That is how you know you have successfully completed this exercise. Your unconscious mind does not understand the difference between a scenario that is genuinely real and a scenario that is vividly imagined. For that reason, vividly imagining confidence in your future means you are literally programming yourself to have that confidence when you need it.

Set a Trigger for the Confidence You've Rehearsed

Here is how to set yourself up to have confidence any time:

1. Close your eyes.
2. Watch yourself on your mental movie screen being confident.
3. Enhance the visual and sound qualities of the movie.
4. Jump into your on-screen body and see through your own eyes, hear what you hear, and feel that total confidence.

5. Hold your thumb and first finger together as you experience confidence.
6. The more you feel confident, the harder you press your thumb and first finger together.
7. After five seconds, separate your thumb and first finger and open your eyes.
8. Repeat the first seven steps, but watch a different confident scenario.

By doing this, you will have programmed your mind to respond to the feeling of your thumb and forefinger pressed together as a confidence trigger. Now that you've rehearsed it, whenever you need confidence you can just close your eyes and press your thumb and forefinger together long enough to let the feeling you've triggered come flooding through you.

Rehearse Confidence

1. Focus on an image of you acting confidently, as on a movie screen.
2. Listen to yourself speaking confidently.
3. View the picture in a close-up, and turn up the volume.
4. Feel the confidence that you project on-screen.

▶ TECHNIQUE 3: Program Confidence

You and I have all the resources we could ever need to be totally successful and unstoppably confident. Many people discount how resourceful they could potentially be. To have unstoppable confidence in the future, the key is to be able to summon your confidence resources at will to get the results you want. You did it successfully in the past, which means you can do it successfully any time. It is only a matter of practice before you have that confidence whenever you choose to switch it on.

Remember a time when you were unstoppably confident in the past. Become aware of what specifically you see, hear, and feel inside as you reexperience what it's like to be completely confident. There is a structure to your confidence experience in the same way that there is a structure to a building. There are certain qualities that you see, hear, and feel in a building that are specific to that building. Similarly, there are certain things you see, hear, and feel only when you are in a confident state. While you relive a past time when you were confident, ask yourself the following questions to become aware of the visual qualities of confidence:

- What size is what you see?
- Do you see a picture or a movie?
- Is it three-dimensional?
- How clear or fuzzy is it?
- How bright is it?
- How close is it?
- Is it in color or in black and white?

Ask yourself the following questions to become aware of the auditory qualities confidence has for you:

- What do you hear?
- How loud is it?
- What is the tempo?
- What is the pitch?
- What direction does the sound come from?

Ask yourself the following questions to become aware of the sensory qualities of confidence:

- Where does the feeling begin in your body?
- How intense is the feeling?
- What direction does the feeling come from?
- How long does the feeling last?

By altering the visual, auditory, and sensory qualities of confidence, you can actually amplify your confident state. Practice playing around with all of these different qualities (see the Appendix for more qualities) and notice the resulting effects on your confident state. This means you can build an even more confident state once you find the qualities that work best for you.

As you relive your past confident experience and become aware of all the visual, auditory, and sensory qualities associated with that experience, realize that you can use these same qualities to program yourself to have unlimited confidence in the future. The way to do this is by imagining situations in the future where you will need unstoppable confidence and imagining your future confident self adjusting what you see, hear, and feel to match your past experience of confidence.

You are literally programming your mind to have unstoppable confidence in the future. When the moment arrives, your mind will act as if you've already experienced it before and give you unlimited confidence. As I've said, the mind does not make a distinction between what is real and what has been *vividly imagined*. Real-time scans of the brain reveal that whether you take a physical action or simply vividly imagine doing it, the same areas of your brain are activated. You can take advantage of this by programming your mind in advance.

Program Confidence

1. Relive a past experience in which you felt confident.
2. Notice all the visual, auditory, and sensory qualities associated with that experience.
3. Imagine a situation in the future where you will need confidence.
4. Imagine yourself adjusting what you see, hear, and feel to match your past experience of confidence.

TECHNIQUE 4: Anchoring

Many who have studied psychology will be aware of the groundbreaking experiments conducted by the animal behaviorist Ivan Pavlov to determine the power of stimulus-response conditioning. After noticing that dogs salivate when they eat, he paired a unique stimulus, the shining of a light, with the presentation of the dog's meal. Pavlov would turn on the light immediately before giving the dog food. After several rounds of this, the dog would salivate even when the light was turned on but no food was presented. Prior to this pairing, shining the light had had no effect on the dog's salivation, but after the stimulus (the light) had been paired with the response (salivation) the dog would reliably salivate when a light was shone.

The phenomenon of stimulus–response conditioning has come to be known in many circles as "anchoring." An anchor is a stimulus that triggers a mental state. It has been applied to phobia treatment, motivation, and other areas of personal development. The beauty of anchoring is that it can be very easy to do for yourself.

Properties of good anchors are that they:

1. Elicit a strong emotional state
2. Must be unique
3. Must be repeatable

Now, it's all very well to work yourself into an unstoppably confident state manually when you have the time, but what about when you'd like to get into that state instantly? This is where anchoring comes in. When you get yourself into the state of being confident, motivated, and strong, you can easily pair that state with a stimulus of your own. Many people like to use music. If you want to do this, pick a piece of music that matches and maybe even evokes the state you want to anchor, such as "Eye of the Tiger" or the *Chariots of Fire* theme.

Pick out one of your favorite confidence techniques and do it along with the music. Do this over and over again, and you will find that just listening to that music immediately plunges you into that state.

You can even anchor states with internal stimuli. Any image that automatically puts you into a certain state is already an anchor. For some people, just thinking about the smiling face of their spouse puts them in a romantic state. Thinking about a happy baby is enough to make many people melt with tenderness.

All of these mental techniques are designed for tapping into your natural power to activate the emotional circuitry of your brain and body to produce a confident state. Once you have that state, you can pair it with outside stimuli like music or pictures, or you can associate it with internal stimuli like remembered images, sounds, or feelings.

The following is a great internal anchor of mine that I want to pass on. After you imagine it a few times, you'll naturally associate what you see and hear inside your mind with a powerfully confident state.

Picture a jet-black puma at the top of a glorious canyon that spans miles across. The puma radiates intensity; its back is arched and it is poised to pounce on its unsuspecting prey below. The prey does not even realize what will transpire as the puma knowingly licks its sharp teeth. As you watch this scene, if you will, step into the puma's body and become the puma. See through the puma's eyes, hear what the puma hears, and feel that unstoppably confident state the puma has as you become completely aware of just how easily you are going to devour your prey (accomplish your goal). To even more fully experience this confident state, let loose with a

GROWWWLLL that will rival any puma alive. Doing this will help to associate this powerful state with the sound of the growl.

After you do this exercise, you will be able to simply growl internally and immediately go back into a state of unstoppable confidence. All you will ever need to do to get there again is stop for a moment, close your eyes, growl (inside your mind), and become the puma.

Anchoring

1. Practice a favorite confidence-generating exercise.
2. While doing so, listen to a piece of music that makes you feel confident or imagine an image that makes you feel good about yourself.
3. When you want to re-create the confident feeling, internally hear that music or see that image.

▶ TECHNIQUE 5: Circle of Confidence

The next technique is an advanced form of anchoring called the "circle of confidence." Instead of anchoring something to a location on your body or to an internal stimulus, this technique anchors confidence to a spot on the ground. In doing so, you will physically step into unstoppable confidence whenever you need it.

There have been times in your past when you were confident. In the future, you will be confident again. The key is to be able to summon that feeling at will. This technique allows you to invoke a state of confidence whenever you want.

To form your circle of confidence, imagine a circular location on the floor. Before you step into the circle, notice its exact dimensions and picture it either with colors or transparent, if you will. When you physically step into the circle, you will move back in time to a moment in which you had complete confidence.

Pick an experience of ultimate confidence. While you are standing in your circle, fully relive that instance of confidence. See what you saw at the time, hear what you heard, and allow yourself to feel the unstoppable confidence of that experience.

Inside the circle and feeling confident, adjust your body language to match your confident state. Keep this confident state with you as you walk around outside the circle.

If you have enough confidence to meet your outcome, you are done with the exercise. If you need more, go back into your circle and relive a different, equally powerful confident experience. Continue stacking up your confidence until you have all you need.

Regardless of wherever you are, you can use your circle of confidence to instantly gain more confidence. Exaggerate your strong, powerful physiology as you train your body how to stand and move. Pretty soon, you will find yourself naturally standing confidently as a habit.

Circle of Confidence

1. Imagine a circle on the ground.
2. Remember a situation in which you felt confident.
3. Relive that experience as you step into the circle.
4. Adopt a confident posture.
5. Step outside the circle and continue to walk and act confidently.

▶ TECHNIQUE 6: Mirror Affirmations

Typically when people do affirmations, they repeat them endlessly in hopes that they will work. Doing so is somewhat effective, but it can be made much more effective with some simple modifications. This technique will supercharge the efficacy of the affirmations. Instead of using statements beginning with "I," you will use statements beginning with "You." These statements are more powerful because they allow your conscious mind to tell *you*—your unconscious mind—specifically what you want, and how to behave.

Get in front of a mirror, stand with confident physiology, and project your intention for these affirmations to change your life. The larger the mirror, the better it is, because you can see more of yourself. With your shoulders back, your head held high, and your stomach sucked in, look yourself squarely in the eye and say the following affirmations:

- "You are completely powerful."
- "You are unstoppably confident."
- "You are becoming more and more confident each and every day."
- "Nothing can stop you."
- "You go for what you want and you get it."

Repeat these affirmations to yourself in the mirror until you can totally feel them in your body. Perhaps you'll see yourself a bit differently, as if you already noticed yourself having more confidence. Or maybe you'll hear your inner voice speaking forcefully with absolute confidence from within. Do this daily as part of your confidence-building regimen and I can guarantee you that you will have unstoppable confidence in little time.

Mirror Affirmations

1. Stand in front of the mirror.
2. Adopt confident physiology (shoulders back, head up, stomach tucked in).
3. Deliver affirmations to yourself in the mirror, using "you" instead of "I" statements.

⟫ TECHNIQUE 7: Future Success Now!

If you were to taste your future success and feel what it would be like to achieve your goals now, wouldn't you feel tremendously more motivated to go for it right now? This "future success now" technique does exactly that. It brings all the future feelings of success into your heart, mind, and soul right now. You will experience such an overwhelming sense of success that you will surrender to your passion and go for it. Any fears you might have had may still be present, but with the desire for success dominating all other emotions, you will feel the need to take action and fulfill your goals.

In this exercise, the outcome you will want to set is to increase your confidence. This means saying, either aloud or inside your mind, "I'm doing this exercise to increase my confidence and feel more passion, which will naturally cause me to go after all my goals and make my dreams a reality." Are you ready to feel your future success?

Close your eyes and picture your mental movie screen. See yourself at the point where you are about to reach the pinnacle of your success. While you are watching yourself, make sure that you see yourself in color on a big, bright, and close-up picture. Fill your mind with stereo surround sound and turn the volume up all the way. Just before you reach the pivotal point where all your success is yours, stop the movie you're watching. Ask yourself some questions to clarify why exactly you are going after this success. What is important to you about this success? What's important to you about getting this pleasure? What's important to you about that? Ultimately, what does having this success do for you?

Now restart the movie and witness yourself achieving your goal and getting all the massive success and pleasure you deserve that comes with it. Right as you see yourself on your mental screen fulfilling your goal and experiencing that wonderful feeling of victory, jump into your on-screen body. See through your own eyes as if you are there now, because in your mind you *are*.

Hear the sounds of success. Feel what success is like in every fiber of your being. As the moment comes to a climax, I want you to take all these wonderful feelings and wrap them up. Take those unlimited feelings with you as you jump out of the mental screen back into your physical body, allowing all of those magnificent feelings to ebb and flow.

You've just smelled the sweet scent of your future success. You've tasted the victory. You realize that glory is yours for the taking. It's up to you to take action now and claim what is rightfully yours. As you complete this exercise, write down five immediate actions you will take that will bring you one step closer to achieving that success that you deserve.

Future Success Now

1. On your mental screen play a movie of you succeeding massively.
2. Just at the point when you are about to get to the peak of your success in the movie, temporarily hit pause.
3. Ask yourself, "What's important about this success? What will having this success do?"
4. Jump into the movie as you begin playing it again. Soak up the unlimited, massive success you know you deserve.
5. When the movie is done, take all of these wonderful feelings back with you and open your eyes.
6. Write down five immediate actions you will take that will bring you one step closer to achieving your goals.

▶ TECHNIQUE 8: Put Your Life in Perspective

Consider whatever appears overwhelming to you now. By the end of the exercise, you will think about it completely differently and have much more confidence about what you're going to do.

Picture a line representing your lifetime. Your past is off to the left, your present is in the center, and your future is off to the right. Now place whatever is bothering you on the timeline and visualize it as a small dot. In your mind, take a step back so you can see a larger portion of your entire timeline instead of just the present. Notice how this puts that minor nuisance into a different perspective? Now mentally step back even further to notice all of your past and all of your future at once, and recognize just how small and insignificant this dot representing your current problem is.

When you keep things in perspective, it's really difficult to waste valuable time and energy on trivial things. The trouble begins when people do not keep the big picture in sight and magnify some issue to be larger than it really is.

Put Your Life in Perspective

1. Visualize your life as a timeline.
2. Picture whatever is overwhelming you as a point on that timeline.
3. Mentally step back to see that dot in perspective.

▶ TECHNIQUE 9: Avoid the Future You Don't Want

As we saw earlier, people are motivated either by moving toward pleasure or by moving away from pain. If we were bunny rabbits, it would be the equivalent of us moving toward carrots or away from people's boots. This next technique will work best for people who run away from the boots, so to speak, because it amplifies the pain of not going after your dreams to the point where it will seem easier to just do it.

To do this exercise, visualize the timeline from Technique 8. Close your eyes and imagine floating above the timeline, drifting forward far into your future. Continue floating forward in time until you get to the point when you are older and most of your opportunities have passed you by. As you get to that point, see yourself on your mental movie screen walking around and feeling miserable. In doing this, you might realize that you are looking at a person who has lived a life unfulfilled.

Tune into the sounds that are coming from that older person who had so much potential, yet somehow failed to take action and live his or her dreams. Just as the feeling of disappointment rises to an extreme and your future self appears to realize that his or her life has not been invested wisely, jump right into that older person's body and see what that experience is like. Feel how awful it is to lead a life unfulfilled.

It's really quite tragic, isn't it? When you fully experience that feeling of deep regret—all the pain, disappointment, and frustration that you *will* feel if you don't go after your dreams by immediately taking action—jump back into your physical body. If you don't take action now to go after your dreams, that is how you will feel when you get older. Since you've experienced the pain that will happen if you don't go after it right now, are you aware of how much more motivated you are to avoid that feeling and live your dreams?

If you hesitate in the future, call up that horrible feeling from this experience and allow that to propel you to take action. To break out of the negative state of mind induced by this exercise, use one of the previous visualization techniques to see the wonderful future you will have when you use your confidence resources to get the future you want!

Avoid the Future You Don't Want

1. Visualize the timeline from Technique 8.
2. See yourself further down the timeline, with most of your opportunities passed over.
3. Imagine your response—physically, audibly, emotionally—to an unfulfilled life.
4. Come back to your present self, and summon those feelings of disappointment and rage when you need motivation.

▶ TECHNIQUE 10: Build an Enriched Past

Oftentimes a lack of confidence when facing a new experience stems from not having done it before. In order to get good at doing something, usually you have to do it poorly at first. But when that happens, some people equate the poor performance with failure and become anxious. Understand that we don't have to do everything perfectly from the start. Having said that, though, how much more confident would you feel if you knew that you *had* done something many times before? I'm willing to bet you would be tremendously more confident. This next technique builds memories from your past that feature you succeeding wildly at whatever it is you're about to do.

You may or may not have heard of false-memory syndrome. False-memory syndrome occurs when someone gets someone else to create memories of events that didn't really happen. However, the false memories are so vividly imagined that they seem real to the person in whom they are implanted—and consequently the person acts as if they are.

In situations like this, the memories are usually disempowering. What if we were to create false memories of ourselves having massive success at what we're really about to do for the first time? How much more confidence will you have when you do this?

Build into your past as many successes as you find necessary. You will do this by visualizing success at what you're about to do and imagining that it happened in the past. As you create your past successes, really intensify the experience so that you catch the feeling of confidence that you need.

When I was starting out in public speaking, I had no experience at all. Since I needed to rapidly gain experience to be credible, I went back into my past and created an entire series of memories. Even though I consciously knew they were false memories, they were so vividly imagined that my unconscious mind knew no difference, which consequently allowed me to behave as if I had already been speaking a lot. I imagined that I had an entire history of making wonderful speeches, motivating audiences, and receiving standing ovations for my abilities. To go one step further, I imagined people taking my message to heart, acting on it, and transforming their lives.

By creating all of these memories, by the time I got up to actually speak for the first time it was delightfully simple, and I radiated confidence from the beginning. Anyone can use these techniques to better himself or herself. It's just a matter of knowing the techniques and applying them to your life.

Build an Enriched Past

1. See yourself in your past, on your mental movie screen, massively succeeding at whatever you are actually about to do for the first time.
2. Crank up all the visual and sound qualities to make the new "memory" really intense.
3. Do this ten times to create ten different positive "memories" of your success.

▶ TECHNIQUE 11: Correct Past Mistakes

This technique goes back into the past and implants new memories in a similar fashion to the exercise in Technique 10. Only this time, instead of giving yourself a history, you will be rewriting your history.

Go back to a time when you really blew it. Perhaps something you were expected to accomplish was not the smashing success you intended it to be. Close your eyes and watch yourself on the mental movie screen as you are just about to make the mistake or screw things up.

Just prior to the instant in time when you're about to start deviating from your success path and start making mistakes, stop the movie. We stop the movie now because we don't want you rehearsing the negative incident, for that only reinforces it as a way of behaving. While the movie is stopped, think about how the situation ideally would have turned out if you could give it any ending.

Restart the movie and replace the old ending with the ideal ending. See, hear, and feel yourself succeeding in the way you deserve. After you've watched the movie from start to finish from a third-person point of view, jump into your on-screen body and run the movie from start to finish— with the new, ideal ending—as you see, hear, and feel that massive success that is yours.

Now, run the entire movie from start to finish ten times. This will recode the past incident as a success in your mind. Furthermore, rehearsing and reinforcing success teaches your mind to create success in the future.

As you look back on your past, you'll notice things feel different. Your past has been enriched and you'll discover yourself moving through the world more resourcefully. One neat thing about this technique is its versatility: you can correct any part of your past in whatever way you want.

Correct Past Mistakes

1. Watch yourself in the past on your mental movie screen, right up to the point just before you made a mistake.
2. At that point, stop the movie and think about what the ideal ending would be.
3. Finish the movie with the ideal solution: you behaving resourcefully and getting your outcome.
4. Run the movie from start to finish with the new ending, feeling what it's like to get your outcome.
5. Jump into your on-screen body and run the movie of the success ten times to lock it in.

▶ TECHNIQUE 12: The Domino Effect

As you recall from earlier in the book, beliefs come in two different forms: causality and meaning ("X causes Y" or "X means Y"). Understanding how beliefs are structured means that we can consciously choose those beliefs that are most empowering to us. For example, if someone believes "public speaking means it's time to be fearful and lack confidence," then obviously this belief will be made manifest in that person's behavior, as he or she gets nervous before making a speech. It's necessary to understand how beliefs are formed to use this next technique.

Think of something that is so far outside your comfort zone that you would be absolutely amazed, surprised, and delighted if you actually did it. In thinking about this, keep in mind that it should be something that is feasible and that you could immediately do, should you make that decision to take action. Become aware of what specifically you would see, hear, and feel when doing it. Now, ponder what sort of confidence it would take for you to do this thing that you are so afraid of.

Once you've thought of something completely outside your comfort zone, you will naturally realize that if you were to actually do this, you could do anything you wanted in the world. After all, if you can step so far outside your comfort zone, you can continue to expand even further outside it, can't you? To make this exercise really work, lock in the belief that doing whatever it is you are thinking of right now that you are afraid to do means that you can do anything.

I chose skydiving as my activity for this exercise. I had led a pretty conservative lifestyle, keeping risks to a bare minimum, and so I had never done anything so daring before.

Some risks, I soon learned, are worth it. To gain more confidence in myself, I built in this belief: "As I jump out of an airplane and hurtle to the ground at rapid speeds, I will be stepping far outside my comfort zone. And by proving to myself that I can do things I wasn't quite sure I could do means that I can do anything in this world." For me, skydiving demonstrated that anything is possible for me. When you do your activity, you'll realize that anything is possible for you.

Your example can be whatever you want it to be, as long as it is a big stretch outside your comfort zone. It could be marching into your boss's office and asking for a raise, speaking in public, or running a marathon. The most important part is that when you make it happen, you will realize that anything is possible for you when you set your mind to it.

When you've decided on what you're going to do, take immediate action to ensure that it will happen. Get things in motion as soon as you can. Taking immediate action is an excellent habit to develop. The most successful, unstoppably confident people take immediate action and accordingly manifest their dreams sooner.

To anyone who is very logical or critically oriented, the belief that "since I can skydive, I can do anything" is not very logical at all. Yet holding the belief that you can do anything will enable you to go for much, much more than those who have limited themselves with logic. You may not be able to do "anything," but you will definitely go past your old limits.

Remember, what seems like a limit is very often just a limit in belief, not reality. When you choose your new beliefs, choose them because they are useful and empowering, not based on so-called logic. Choose your new beliefs because they will help you live your dreams.

The Domino Effect

1. Choose an activity that is far outside your comfort zone.
2. Realize that in doing that activity, you make it possible to do anything you choose to do.
3. Follow through on this activity as quickly as possible.
4. Hold on to the new belief that you can make anything happen.

▶ TECHNIQUE 13: Borrow Confidence

A great way to gain confidence is to model yourself after someone else who already has a lot of confidence. Anyone who has an absolute belief in himself or herself will make a good model for you. One way to supercharge your results using this technique is to repeat it, using several different people as your models of unstoppable confidence.

Once you've identified the person who embodies confidence to you, get to know as thoroughly as possible how this person moves through the world. To do this, spend as much time as you can with the person and talk about his or her opinions on confidence, life, and taking action. If your model of confidence is not accessible to you, perhaps you can get to know the person vicariously by purchasing his or her books, CDs, or home-study courses, or by attending a seminar. If it's a rock star, you could go to his or her concert. If it's a star athlete, perhaps you could attend his or her sporting event. The idea here is to expose your mind to this person as much as possible. The better grasp you have on your model's beliefs, attitudes, and values, the more effectively you can model his or her confidence.

Set a strong outcome for this exercise, such as: "I want confidence like [name your model of confidence] for these reasons: [list the reasons]." By the time you reach this point, you have already familiarized yourself with your model of confidence and have a good grasp on his or her perceptions of the world, the self, and what he or she does.

Close your eyes and envision your model of confidence behaving in an unstoppably confident way in a movie on your mental screen. Pay close attention to how the person speaks, moves, gestures, and walks. Become aware of how this person interacts with others, imagine his or her internal self-talk, and notice anything else you can about the person. Make the movie big, bright, and close. Turn the sound up all the way so that it resonates in you.

Next, step into the movie as if you are stepping into your confidence model's body. Take on this person's entire being. See as though you are seeing through your confidence model's eyes, hear with his or her ears, and feel what it is like to completely immerse yourself and be as unstoppably confident as this person.

While you are inside your confidence model's shoes, physically do all you can to be like this person. Gesture, speak, move, and use the same facial expressions your model does. Continue doing this until you fully understand what it feels like to have your model's unstoppable confidence.

If it helps, imagine yourself as this person in different contexts. When you fully have that feeling down, see yourself stepping outside of the person's body and back into yours. As you float back into your own body, take with you that unstoppably confident feeling you've just created. Integrate that feeling into your body, your mind, and your identity. By having your model's confidence once, you can have it any time you want simply by doing this exercise.

Borrow Confidence

1. Find someone whose confidence you'd like to have for yourself.
2. Expose yourself to that model of confidence as much as possible.
3. Watch your role model behaving confidently on your mental movie screen. Notice how this person moves through the world, how he or she speaks and gestures.
4. Make the image really compelling by turning up the visual, auditory, and sensory qualities.
5. Step into the movie and become the model. Gesture, speak, and move through the world as this person does with this unstoppable confidence.
6. Step into the model in five different contexts.
7. When you feel you have a handle on this person's confidence, step outside the model's body and take his or her confidence back with you.

TECHNIQUE 14: Schedule Your Dreams

Successful people plan their work and then work their plan. This technique will help you decide on what you want and focus your energy toward pursuing it. Goals are dreams with deadlines. For that reason, this technique gives you some specific deadlines for achieving your dreams.

What I want you to do is imagine yourself five years in the future, living your ideal lifestyle. What sort of job do you have? What have you accomplished? Where do you live? What is your lifestyle like? Focus in on the answers to these questions. Once you have the answers, build what I call an "expanded résumé."

A typical résumé charts what you have accomplished and the skills you possess now. The expanded résumé encompasses your entire life: your family life, your career, your social circle, your spirituality, your finances, and so on. Create an expanded résumé that will be true for you in five years. Reread this résumé once a week—or more often, if you can invest the time—and in five years' time, you will have accomplished much, if not all, of what you put down.

A similar technique for channeling your energy into the direction you want is to construct a future magazine cover—with yourself on it. The magazine could be either real or fictitious, but it should show you succeeding in whatever area of life you choose. When I did this, I used computer presentation software to import my photograph, design the magazine cover, and insert catchy headlines that described what I would achieve. When the cover was finished, I printed it out and proudly displayed it on my desk. From time to time, I still glance over at my desk to find it there, and I automatically become more motivated to take action and move toward my goals.

Schedule Your Dreams

The Expanded Résumé

1. Imagine where you'd like to be five years from now.
2. Write down the details: family, work, leisure time, friends, and so on.
3. Review this expanded résumé at least once a week.

Your Future Magazine Cover

1. Create a real or imagined magazine cover with yourself on it succeeding in some area of your life.
2. Use catchy headlines and images to describe what you want to achieve.
3. Review your magazine cover periodically to keep you motivated in reaching your goals.

▶ TECHNIQUE 15: Swish into Confidence

The next technique is called the "swish" technique because in it, you redirect your brain as rapidly as a basketball makes the "swish" sound when it flies through the net. Our minds are trained to go in a certain direction. Sometimes, if we have not been consciously directing our minds, we tend to gravitate toward less-than-resourceful behaviors, such as shyness. This technique redirects the brain, in effect telling it, "Not shy: confident!"

If you act shy, you do it out of a pattern you've either consciously or unconsciously set up for yourself. There are triggers that cue you to begin the shyness pattern. What we're going to do is to take those same triggers and retrain your mind so that they spur you toward confidence instead.

Think of the times when you act shy. Decide on what the initial cue is that lets you know it's time to get nervous and tentative. For some people, arriving at a party full of strangers and looking at their unfamiliar faces is a cue to begin acting shy. For others, seeing an attractive member of the opposite sex sit down nearby sets them off. Find out what your cue is. People do not randomly become shy. There is always a cue that precedes it.

Now that you've discovered the cue that has led you to shyness in the past, put yourself into the picture and experience it from a first-person perspective. Practice making the picture of what you see smaller, darker, and farther away. Take the normal picture—the cue image—and make it small, dark, and really far away in the time it takes you to say out loud, "Swish!" Do this until you feel you can take the picture of your shyness cue and make it disappear in an instant.

Following that, picture an image of your ideal self, but don't "jump into" the image yet. Picture yourself and how you want to behave, instead of how you currently do. See those strong, confident gestures, facial expressions, and posture, and make sure that when you think about your ideal self, you feel really motivated to be that way. If you don't feel a strong sense of motivation, then adjust the image of your ideal self until you do. Make this picture small, dark, and far away at first, and practice making the picture really big, bright, and close as rapidly as you can say out loud, "Swish!" Practice this exercise until you can do it easily.

Now what we're going to do is redirect your mind so that whenever it experiences the cue image, it will automatically flash to your ideal self and therefore draw you into being that person. When you've done this successfully, you will see the trigger that used to make you shy and immediately experience an unconscious shift into confidence.

Close your eyes and see the cue image in the forefront of your mind. See it big, bright, and close up, just like you would if you were experiencing it for real. In the lower right-hand corner of your vision, see your ideal self-image as smaller, darker, and farther away. Make the "swish" sound, and simultaneously flip the two pictures so that the cue image becomes small, dark, and far away as the ideal self-image becomes really big, bright, and close. Remember to make the "swish" sound as you do this exercise because it will help you unconsciously move the pictures around.

Pause for a moment, open your eyes, and then reset the pictures so that you see the cue image big and close and your confident self in the lower right-hand corner. Then make the "swish" sound as you transpose them in the same way you did previously.

Continue to repeat this pausing, resetting, and "swish-
ing" of pictures until simply looking at the cue image automatically triggers your brain to gravitate toward your ideal
self-image. That's how you know you've been successful in
retraining your mind.

Swish into Confidence

1. Identify the cue that triggers your shyness.
2. Practice making the image of that cue smaller, darker, and
   farther away until you can do it in the time it takes to say
   "swish."
3. Now picture your idealized self smaller, darker, and farther
   away.
4. Practice making that idealized self bright and close up,
   again in the time it takes to say "swish."
5. Finally, practice transposing the two pictures, so that at the
   sound of the word "swish," your brain will make the shyness
   trigger small and far away while bringing your idealized self
   to the forefront.

TECHNIQUE 16: Dissociate, Add Resources, Act Differently

Sometimes people feel overwhelmed by situations because they are too deeply invested in them. If someone is too close to the situation, it may be difficult for him or her to reason logically about it. For example, if you have to make a major decision and there is an overriding emotional component, that emotional component may skew your judgment. This technique helps you stand back and survey the big picture in order to make the best decision for yourself.

What you will do in this technique is to observe yourself in a third-person point of view; you will step outside your body and look over at yourself making a decision. Picture yourself on your mental movie screen, but don't "jump into" your on-screen body. You are a detached observer. Pretend that you are the narrator as you refer to yourself in the third person by repeatedly using your name.

Think through the decision-making process out loud in a detached frame of mind. As you narrate your thinking process regarding the decision, be sure you have confident physiology and tonality. This will help you make a firm commitment to the decision at which you ultimately arrive. As a result, your decision will be more rational, and emotion will have less influence over your decision, since you have literally given yourself some distance from the situation.

Another way to perform this technique is with the confidence resource triangle, described next. The main difference is that the triangle uses physical locations to represent the different states.

The confidence resource triangle has three legs: a "stuck-state" location, a "dissociated-observer" location, and a "resource" location. The stuck state is the state where a person will experience indecision and need a resource. The dissociated location is where a person can stand back and objectively look at the situation from a third-person point of view. The resource location represents a resource that will get a person unstuck from his or her indecisive state.

Find three different spots on the floor and label one "S" for *stuck*, one "D" for *dissociated*, and one "R" for *resource*. First, step onto the "S" location. Close your eyes if it helps you. See, hear, and feel all the elements of a context where you need more confidence. Just when you've gotten a taste of it, step outside the location.

Name three different things in the room to break your state and thus get you out of your stuck state.

Second, step onto the "D" location. Look at the same situation you did in the "S" location, but do it from a third-person perspective. Notice how it's different and that you can perceive things more objectively. Think of a confidence resource that would help you conquer this stuck state.

Third, step onto the "R" location. As you do this physical step, you will mentally step into the resource by completely reliving a past time when you were confident. See what you saw, hear what you heard, and feel what it's like to really crank up your confidence level.

Now, with this overwhelming confidence at your disposal, step back into what used to be the stuck state. How easily and naturally do you get unstuck now, with all this confidence oozing from every fiber of your being?

If for some reason your stuck state did not change for you as much as you would have liked, do the exercise again; continue stacking up confident resources and bringing them to the stuck state until things change.

Dissociate, Add Resources, Act Differently

1. Envision yourself in a stuck location.
2. Step out of the stuck location and name three things in the room to balance yourself.
3. Step into the dissociated location and watch how you resolve this situation in a confident manner.
4. Step into the resource location and think back to a time in your life when you exuded confidence.

▶ TECHNIQUE 17: Matching and Mirroring

When two people have rapport with each other, an interesting thing occurs. Their body language becomes similar and they begin to match each other. How can we use this to our benefit? We can consciously match someone else's body language in order to increase our perceived similarity to that person. You can use matching to increase intimacy in almost any human interaction.

This technique is called matching and mirroring because your goal is to become a mirror image of your partner in conversation. When I first learned this technique, I confused it with mimicking. Mimicking is something that young children do to annoy their parents, or monkeys do to play with visitors at the zoo. We are not mimicking anyone else. Instead, we are increasing our similarity to another person by mirroring that person's body language, which will help engender a greater understanding of his or her point of view.

The way to match and mirror someone is to adopt the same body posture as that person has. When the person moves, you move with him or her. Be sure to allow for a certain lag time so that your matching does not creep into the person's conscious awareness. The idea is to gain rapport at an unconscious level, without attracting notice to what you are doing. The intended effect is that the other person will feel that you are similar to him or her, without being quite sure why. As your rapport deepens, you can trim the lag time until pretty soon you are moving exactly with the person.

Rapport is like a dance; one person leads and one person follows. Up until this point, you've been involved in the dance and only been following. After sufficient rapport has been established, you now have an opportunity to lead the dance of rapport. To begin leading, move your body into a new position and see if the other person follows you. When the person does follow, you will know that you are now the one in charge. If you move and the person does not follow you, go back to matching and mirroring to build up the rapport further. While you lead nonverbally, you can match and mirror people in other ways.

In addition to matching body language, you can match people's breathing too. This practice will serve to unconsciously synchronize you and the other person and facilitate rapport. To match someone's breathing, watch his or her shoulders. Most people's shoulders rise when inhaling a breath and fall when exhaling. People exhale as they are talking, so remember to match someone's breathing as the person speaks. The more similar you are to another person, even in barely perceptible behaviors such as breathing, the deeper the rapport you will create.

As well as matching someone's breathing, you can match hand gestures as well. When the other person is talking, notice how he or she gestures. No matter whether someone has wild, demonstrative gestures, or slight, precise hand gestures, match the person when it is your turn to speak by using the same gestures. I don't care if it feels awkward or if it's outside your comfort zone. You are matching the other person in order to better understand and communicate with him or her.

Facial expressions are another great way to match and mirror someone to develop greater rapport. Smiling, frowning, raising of the eyebrows, or any other facial expression can be matched. You can even match someone's muscle tone. If the person is uptight and stressed out, you can tighten yourself up. If the person is loose and relaxed, you can act the same way to be with him or her in the moment. Suppose you match someone who is tense. You can develop great rapport with the person and then begin to lead the dance of rapport by gradually relaxing. If the rapport is sufficient, the person will follow you and relax as well.

The level of perceived similarity between you and another person is directly proportional to the rapport you will experience. The greater the level of rapport you experience, the more freedom you will have to relax and be your own confident self around the person.

A good rule of communication is to remember that nobody is going to get your message across for you, so do whatever it takes to make sure you are heard. Nonverbally matching someone can help facilitate this and increase the chances that your message is received the way you intended it. It's not up to the other person to make sure he or she gets it. As an excellent communicator, it's solely up to you to share your message loud and clear.

Matching and Mirroring

1. With a friend, practice mirroring his or her movements.
2. First, adopt the same body posture your friend has.
3. Next, match your friend's gestures.
4. Third, mirror your friend's facial expressions.
5. When you are aware that rapport has been deepened, try making your own gestures or facial expressions and see if your friend matches your movements.

▶ TECHNIQUE 18: Verbal Matching

You now understand how to create rapport by nonverbally matching someone. Of course, you can further deepen rapport by matching someone verbally as well. Typical verbal behaviors you can match are tone of voice, volume of voice, rate of speech, inflection (for example, questioning or commanding), and word usage. If someone speaks rapidly, for example, you shouldn't speak much more slowly. You want to keep up with that person's speech rate. If someone speaks slowly, you don't want to be a motormouth when talking with that person. You want to speak at near the same rate the person is speaking.

Listen to people's key words—the words they say over and over again. I like to call them their "trigger" or "hot button" words. When you hear these words, use them right back and notice how your rapport skyrockets. My trigger words are sprinkled throughout this book. If we were to meet, and you spoke with me using some of the more prevalent words in this book, you would notice how delighted I became, and our rapport would skyrocket. Some of my trigger words are *unstoppable, fun, powerful, delight,* and *awesome.*

Here's an example of how to match someone's trigger words. The conversation is between an artist and her friend. The artist may say, "I like my art because it's expressive and freeing. I get to be myself. I paint landscapes that are breathtaking and wide open. It allows me to express myself in a way that I didn't get to before. Painting is liberating because I can see the beauty of things around me and express them to others."

The friend could match the numerous trigger words by saying, "That makes sense. I understand where you're coming from. It seems like it would be liberating to really let loose and express yourself to others. To be able to see the true beauty in things to the point where it takes your breath away is really awesome. I can see why you like painting so much."

The result of this communication will be that rapport has deepened because of all the trigger words the painter used when discussing her passion for painting. Elicit someone's passion, listen for trigger words, and then use those words when speaking with the person. You will be amazed at how quickly you develop excellent rapport.

Verbal Matching

1. To increase rapport, practice verbally matching a friend.
2. First, match your friend's tone and volume of voice.
3. Next, match the rate of speech.
4. Finally, pick up on your friend's trigger words and use them as you respond to what your friend is saying.

TECHNIQUE 19: Parroting

Parrots are interesting birds because they repeat certain words or sentences when they are said frequently enough. By acting like a parrot, we can increase rapport. When someone is speaking and pauses, repeat the last few words of the sentence right back to the person. The person's words have special significance to him or her or they wouldn't have been chosen that way. Be like the parrot and repeat the exact words back.

You'll discover how easily this causes a greater sense of rapport. Parroting validates that person's point of view and demonstrates that you are listening. People like to have their point of view validated and they enjoy being listened to, which is why parroting works so well.

> FRED: How are you doing today?
> CAROLYN: Excellent. I had a flat tire on the way to work but I made it here all right.
> FRED: You made it here all right. How has your workday been since that?
> CAROLYN: It's been pretty hectic around the office. I've got a team meeting this afternoon at 4:00.
> FRED: You've got a team meeting at 4:00. Uh-huh.
> CAROLYN: Yeah, I'm really looking forward to it. The product should be unveiled here really soon.
> FRED: Really soon.
> CAROLYN: Next week is our scheduled launch. We've been working really hard to get this project going.
> FRED: Next week. You must have been working really hard to get this project going.

The parroting is delivered as a mere echo of what the person previously said, with the key points echoed back to the person. The speaker, upon hearing his or her own words parroted back, will either say yes or agree nonverbally, perhaps with a nod. When people are in agreement, they are generally in an excellent state of rapport.

Avoid active listening, which is when you change around what someone said by putting it into your own words and then spewing it back at the person. By changing the words you change the meaning and distort the true message that the person wanted to convey. People like to get their message across, and parroting their exact words back confirms that you've received them.

Parroting

1. With a friend, begin a conversation and practice repeating the last phrase your friend said back to him or her.
2. Make sure not to rephrase in your own words.

TECHNIQUE 20: Nodding, Leaning Forward, and Prodding

People who are masterful communicators nod as they are listening to others. In doing so, they invite others to relax and share whatever is on their mind. The next time you are talking with someone, continually nod to open the person up for sharing.

To practice this, get a partner and have a conversation. Say as little as possible and nod as often as you can. This is what effective communicators do, and by modeling effective communicators, your confidence in interpersonal skills will dramatically increase.

Disinterested communicators lean back and slouch. Excellent communicators lean forward and show that they are hanging on each and every word said. In this exercise, lean forward as you nod along.

As you're talking with your partner, prod him or her on by throwing in the following phrases at the appropriate pauses:

- Uh–huh.
- Go on.
- I understand.
- That makes sense.
- Tell me more.
- I see what you are saying.
- I hear you.
- That feels right to me.

You'll soon discover how effectively this keeps people talking. I've kept people talking for thirty minutes at a time without my saying anything, just by nodding, leaning forward, and interjecting these phrases at the appropriate times.

Nodding, Leaning Forward, and Prodding

1. Ask a friend to begin telling you a story.
2. Practice nodding and prodding at appropriate points in the story.
3. See how long you can keep your friend talking.

▶ TECHNIQUE 21: Ask Open-Ended Questions

When you realize that you can talk to anyone, anywhere, anytime, you will have more confidence in yourself than ever before. A secret to being a great conversationalist is knowing how to ask questions that show genuine interest in the other person. Quite simply, ask open-ended questions whenever possible.

Open-ended questions require more than a simple yes-or-no response. The person answering has to elaborate and describe what he or she is thinking. Closed questions do not further develop conversations, since they are usually followed by short answers. If someone repeatedly responds to you with one-word answers, there's not much to work with in developing the conversation.

An example of a closed question and response is:

BRAD: "How are you doing today?"
EILEEN: "Fine."

An example of an open-ended question and response is:

BRAD: "If anything were possible, what would you most like to be doing right now?"
EILEEN: "I have a passion for sailing. I would love to be sailing my boat around the world with my friends. I've been sailing before and I loved it. I can't wait to go again."

You can see how open-ended and closed questions elicit entirely different responses. As you ask these open-ended questions, be sure to listen intently to what the person is saying. While you are listening to someone, use the other methods taught in this book to develop even greater rapport. You can nod and lean forward, parrot the person's words back to him or her, use nonverbal matching and mirroring, and use trigger words. Doing all of this at once may be cumbersome at first. Therefore, practice each skill individually and when you've mastered them, begin to combine them for even better rapport with others.

Ask Open-Ended Questions

1. Engage a friend in conversation.
2. Ask open-ended questions and see how long you can keep the conversation going.

14

Your Confident Future

Whatever we expect with confidence becomes our own self-fulfilling prophecy.

—Brian Tracy

THIS CHAPTER CONTAINS A FEW final pieces of advice to get you on your way. And once you've started, make sure you don't stop!

Build Your Community

As your confidence grows, others will notice the change within you and perhaps behave differently than before. That's normal. They are used to you acting in a particular way and when you behave differently, they might not have a pattern for interacting with you anymore. They will adapt to your newfound confidence and develop an affinity for it. When I first began breaking out of my shy shell, I was concerned about how others would treat me. Much to my delight, they seemed to enjoy being around me more thoroughly as a direct result of my increased confidence.

Family and Friends

Enlist the support of your friends and family to help you on your confidence journey. When you are behaving in a confident manner, they can compliment you and reinforce the behavior. Tell them that you would appreciate their support as you do these confidence exercises. Similarly, if they catch you falling into your old shy habits, they can politely point that out to you, which means you can immediately correct that behavior.

Some people may have negative reactions to your enhanced confidence and zest for life. They are not your genuine friends. Your genuine friends want the best for you, and anything less means they are not your true friends. If someone tries to criticize your increased confidence, view this as an opportunity to test your confidence and let that criticism bounce right off you without making any impact.

Learning Unstoppable Confidence with Others

In addition, I recommend meeting regularly with other like-minded people to teach unstoppable confidence to others and to increase your own confidence. Let this book serve as a guide while your group does the confidence exercises with each other. Getting together with other people can be an incredibly powerful way to ratchet up your confidence. You can support each other on the journey to greater success.

When you get together with others, you can talk about situations when you were confident and situations where

YOUR CONFIDENT FUTURE

191

you need more confidence. Others may have insights that haven't occurred to you, and you might be able to help them likewise. Meet with these people on a regular basis; once a month would be great. Harness the power of synergy, which is the concept that the whole is greater than the sum of the parts. In the case of your confidence group, the entire group's intelligence exceeds that of each individual's intelligence summed up.

Take Action Now

Your power lies in the present. That means you need to cast off procrastination and do it now, whatever "it" may be. I cannot emphasize this point strongly enough. Dismiss the "it can wait until later" mentality. The sooner you adopt the do-it-now attitude, the sooner you will create better relationships, have more fun in life, and fulfill your dreams.

The reason doing things as soon as you possibly can is easier than procrastinating is because of the psychic weight of the things you put off. If you typically procrastinate on something, you might think to yourself, "I should be doing that instead of this." Then you might talk yourself into doing it later. Meanwhile, the leisure activity, which you were supposed to be enjoying, is now consequently ruined because your mind is preoccupied with what you should be doing. That is why the do-it-now mentality is so powerful. It's really much easier to set up and finish tasks and then, free from your obligations, enjoy yourself in your favorite leisure activity.

The great equalizer among us all is that in each and every day, we all have the same twenty-four hours to invest. Most people don't think of their time as an investment. Once you've spent today's twenty-four hours, you can *never* get them back. *Ever.* People endlessly hang out, wasting time, without ever realizing that time can never be recaptured.

I'm all for leisure and spending quality time with friends and loved ones. My main objection is toward people who are acting without purpose (or rather, being inactive without purpose). If people consciously choose how they spend their time, that is fine.

To maximize your use of your time, survey your life. Find out what wastes your time and eliminate it so you can spend more time doing what you thoroughly enjoy. If something is unbearable to you, hire someone else to do it; or perhaps trade responsibilities with a friend, partner, or spouse. It all comes down to this simple message: do more of what you like and less of what you don't.

The following is an exercise to discover how you invest your time. When you finish it, the results might surprise you. Go through your results and eliminate the time-wasters. Maximize doing what you love. You will find yourself being more efficient in the following weeks, since you will know what tasks consume large chunks of your time and what tasks can be delegated.

1. For an entire week, write down what you are doing every half-hour.
2. At the end of the week, notice what you spend most of your time doing.
3. Ask yourself how easily you can eliminate time-wasting activities.
4. Ask yourself how you can invest more time on the activities that will lead you closer to your goals.
5. Schedule your next week according to what you discover.

As you continue to use your time ever more wisely and productively, notice how this increases your confidence. The more actions you take to make your dreams come true, the more motivated you will feel to do and achieve even more. The proper fruit of knowledge is action. Take action and reap the full benefits of your knowledge.

Stay on Track with Your Confidence Practice Calendar

One method to stay on track as you develop your ability to be confident at will is to make a confidence practice calendar. You can take an ordinary calendar and schedule which confidence exercises you will do on which particular days. You can also set up milestones that you expect to achieve on your journey toward unstoppable confidence and compare your progress against them.

One day you could practice speaking confidently. The next day, the day's exercise could be walking confidently. The following day's exercise could be gesturing confidently. Go through this book, pick out your favorite exercises, and put them down on your calendar. Create the calendar to match your personality; you will know what will work best for you.

Positive reinforcement is a great motivator. Therefore, I recommend that you praise yourself when you find that you're behaving confidently. Although you might think it's a bit corny—I know I did at first—I found that the following reinforcement method really worked. When I found myself behaving in a way that I wanted, I gave myself a small round of applause, a pat on the back, and a self-hug. Many people deny themselves their due credit, even when they perform extraordinarily. Give yourself credit by consciously reinforcing your positive behavior.

After all, who is the only person you are guaranteed to be with for twenty-four hours every day for the rest of your life? You are, of course. Treat yourself well and discover how your unconscious mind responds. As you treat yourself better, you'll discover that you're able to access parts of your memory that you hadn't before, you are able to visualize better, and your negative internal dialogue will disappear.

Many people do not treat themselves very well. They have a nagging internal dialogue making their lives miserable. They think that people are out to get them. People are causes in their lives, not effects.

Disempowered people let things happen to them; empowered people make things. When people take complete responsibility over their lives, they become empowered. They realize they always have a choice, and they act out of conscious decisions instead of blaming others or playing the victim role.

When you are empowered and acting out of choice, celebrate your accomplishments by rewarding yourself. Reward yourself in the same way that you'd reward your best friend for his or her accomplishment. Remind yourself that you are wonderful.

Sometimes people don't celebrate their accomplishments. They stall or wait for others to do it. Maybe they want permission to celebrate what they did. I'm now giving my permission for you to celebrate all of your successes.

Live a Healthy Life

In order to be unstoppably confident, you must lead a healthy, fulfilling life. There are three components that are essential to leading such a life: flexibility, a sense of humor, and an orientation toward the future.

Flexibility

You have flexibility in life when you have enough choices to be able to do what it takes to achieve your outcome. If something does not work, you have the wherewithal to realize that it's not working and adjust your behavior (in other words, use flexibility) until you eventually get your result. The more flexible people are, the more likely they will get what they want.

There is a law of cybernetics, which is the science of effective organization, that states, "The person or component with the most choices in the system wins." Take negotiation, for example. If someone has many options and the opposition has few, the first party has the upper hand. The fewer options you have, the less empowered you are. Maximize your empowerment by being flexible and by having as many options and choices as you can imagine.

A Sense of Humor

Having a sense of humor is essential in life. It means you won't take things too seriously or blow them out of proportion. I'm sure we all know people who take everything too seriously and end up having health problems, or smoking and drinking to escape from their problems. A more useful way of experiencing life is by laughing your way through it. When times are the toughest and you are completely stressed out, the ability to laugh out loud is truly priceless.

Laughing out loud will help to center you, which will lead you into a more resourceful and problem-solving state of mind. People who are excessively serious and overly formal tend to have ulcers, heart attacks, strokes, and other medical maladies because they choose to allow themselves to get stressed out. People who laugh a lot are healthier and live longer. Be sure to keep your sense of humor as you continue on through your life's journey.

Future Orientation

There are three different ways we can orient ourselves with respect to time: the past, the present, and the future. Each can be a useful outlook, but having a strong future orientation is the best path for living your dream life. A past orientation can be useful for summoning positive resources from an earlier period in your life. Some people who are heavily oriented toward the past virtually live in their bygone glory days, however, continually rehashing them through storytelling and other reminiscences. Focusing solely on the past makes it easy for you not to take any action toward building the future.

People who get overly caught up in a present-time orientation live entirely in the moment and fail to plan for the future. This flawed outlook can have dire consequences. These people want immediate gratification without having to think about the negative effects of their decisions. A certain amount of present-time orientation is great for cherishing each moment of your life and allowing for spontaneity, provided that you still plan for the future. The ideal orientation is to balance the future and the present together.

Knowing what you want for the future, planning for it, and taking action—while enjoying yourself along the way—is the ultimate ideal to strive for. By delaying instant gratification, having patience, and diligently working toward your goals as you thrive in the present moment, you will have the ideal time-orientation combination. When you find the balance that works best for you, you'll know it.

Life is short and we don't know what tomorrow holds. We can plan for a wonderful future while we make the most of today. You can achieve your dreams when you take action and work your plan. Life goes by so quickly that we must remind ourselves to cherish each and every moment.

Get Going—and Don't Stop

With your unstoppable confidence, you're going to want to tackle the world at once. When you consider all that you want to and *can* achieve in your lifetime, you might want to go out and do it all right now. You can tackle the world, of course, but you should do it in progressive stages. You will have so many dreams and passions awakened that it may seem overwhelming. Sometimes when people feel overwhelmed, they do nothing because they don't know where to begin. Avoid letting this happen to you.

Consider your most important, immediate goals and pursue those first. Remember to take action each and every day, no matter how much or how little it brings you closer to fulfilling your goals.

A journey of a thousand miles begins with a single step. Focus on taking the next step every day. Beware, though, that if you focus only on the next action as part of a larger goal, you may lose sight of why you're going after the goal in the first place. The ideal here is to have a balance: keep the big picture in mind (remembering what's important to you about the goal and why you're doing it) as you focus on the small steps that actually get you there (taking action each and every day).

Being unstoppably confident means being proactive. Decide what you want, go after it, and get it. Some people say, "Someday it will happen for me," or "I'm waiting for my lucky break." The problem is that these reactive people will be waiting forever. Resourceful people make it happen.

Luck is where preparation meets opportunity. Be prepared and relentlessly pursue the opportunities and you'll surprise yourself at how lucky you become. Go out there and make it happen, because you are unstoppable.

Appendix

Qualities to Alter Your Experience and Your Beliefs

YOU CAN WORK ON ALTERING your experiences by focusing on the following qualities:

Visual Qualities

Color	Is the image in color or black and white?
Size	How big or small is the image?
Detail	How detailed is the image
Focus	How clear is the image?
Contrast	Do the elements of the image contrast?
Brightness	How bright or dull is the image?
Border	Is there a border around the image?

Distance	How near or far away is the image to you?
Shape	What shape is the image?
Location	Where is the image located?
Perspective	From what vantage point do you view the image?
Dimension	Is the image flat or three-dimensional?
Movement	Is the image fixed or is a movie playing?

Auditory Qualities

Location	Where is the sound coming from?
Tonality	What is the tonality like?
Depth	Does the sound surround you?
Volume	How loud or quiet is the sound?
Melody	Is the sound melodic or monotonous?
Duration	Is the sound continuous or intermittent?

Sensory Qualities

Intensity	How intense is the feeling?
Location	Where do you feel the feeling?
Speed	How fast does the feeling occur?
Duration	Is the feeling continuous or intermittent?
Quality	How would you describe the feeling?

Index